GRIEVE
BREATHE
RECEIVE

T0049602

GRIEVE
BREATHE
RECEIVE

Finding a Faith Strong Enough to Hold Us

STEVE CARTER

W Publishing Group

AN IMPRINT OF THOMAS NELSON

Grieve, Breathe, Receive

© 2024 Steve Carter

All rights reserved. No portion of this book may be reproduced, stored in a retrieval system, or transmitted in any form or by any means—electronic, mechanical, photocopy, recording, scanning, or other—except for brief quotations in critical reviews or articles, without the prior written permission of the publisher.

Published in Nashville, Tennessee, by W Publishing, an imprint of Thomas Nelson.

Published in association with The Bindery Agency, www.TheBinderyAgency.com.

Thomas Nelson titles may be purchased in bulk for educational, business, fundraising, or sales promotional use. For information, please email SpecialMarkets@ThomasNelson.com.

Unless otherwise noted, Scripture quotations are taken from the Holy Bible, New International Version®, NIV®. Copyright © 1973, 1978, 1984, 2011 by Biblica, Inc.® Used by permission of Zondervan. All rights reserved worldwide. www.zondervan.com. The "NIV" and "New International Version" are trademarks registered in the United States Patent and Trademark Office by Biblica, Inc.®

Scripture quotations marked KJV are taken from the King James Version. Public domain.

Scripture quotations marked MSG are taken from THE MESSAGE. Copyright © 1993, 2002, 2018 by Eugene H. Peterson. Used by permission of NavPress. All rights reserved. Represented by Tyndale House Publishers, a Division of Tyndale House Ministries.

Scripture quotations marked NASB are taken from the New American Standard Bible® (NASB). Copyright © 1960, 1962, 1963, 1968, 1971, 1972, 1973, 1975, 1977, 1995 by The Lockman Foundation. Used by permission. www.Lockman.org.

Any internet addresses, phone numbers, or company or product information printed in this book are offered as a resource and are not intended in any way to be or to imply an endorsement by Thomas Nelson, nor does Thomas Nelson vouch for the existence, content, or services of these sites, phone numbers, companies, or products beyond the life of this book.

Illustrations by Natalia Warren

ISBN 978-0-7852-3561-3 (softcover)
ISBN 978-0-7852-3562-0 (eBook)
ISBN 978-0-7852-3563-7 (audiobook)

Library of Congress Control Number: 2023951441

Printed in the United States of America
24 25 26 27 28 LBC 5 4 3 2 1

To Sarah, Emerson, and Mercy:
home is wherever I'm with you.

CONTENTS

CONTENTS

PART THREE: RECEIVE

INTRODUCTION

Welcome to Grieve, Breathe, Receive

Years ago, I had the chance to work with two young interns, Dan and Ryan, who were eager to learn all they could about leadership and the experiences of working in a church environment. They would occasionally travel with me to some of my speaking engagements across the country. On one trip, we had a day off between events in Southern California. I'd grown up in California and spent my subsequent college years there, and looked forward to showing them around some of my favorite local spots.

We stopped at a well-known beach called the Wedge and watched brave bodysurfers catch massive waves breaking on the shoreline before heading to one of my favorite places for fish tacos, Bear Flag Fish Co. After consuming our weight in freshly caught panko-crusted white fish smothered in pico de gallo and their world-famous tommy sauce, we found a bookstore and picked up something to read at our next stop in Newport.

After stepping inside and getting our bearings, we split up and began our search for the perfect beach read. What do a pastor and his interns consider a beach read? I was hunting for *The Spirit of the Disciplines* by Dallas Willard,[1] while the guys were looking for something lighter.

After a few minutes of wandering around with no luck, I heard Ryan's voice two aisles over: "Are you finding what you're looking for?"

Who was this guy talking to? I thought. *Is he acting like he works here?* Dan and I headed over to where he was standing. There was a woman beside him, her eyes puffy. I looked up and realized we were standing in the "Grief and Loss" section of the bookstore. As my eyes grazed the shelves, I noticed they seemed especially sparse.

"Well, actually . . . no, I'm not," the woman replied, looking down and shuffling her feet. I could tell by her tone and body language she was uncomfortable and overwhelmed.

Ryan asked, "What are you looking for? Maybe I can help." I felt immensely proud of him at that moment. It takes considerable empathy to make room and offer to help someone struggling.

She heaved a weary sigh and responded, "I don't know how to grieve. I mean, I don't know how to go through this alone. My twenty-one-year-old son died unexpectedly six months ago, and I'm still completely lost."

Ryan glanced at me and waved me in. He introduced

me to the woman, whose name I learned was Rose. I told her I had been a pastor for several years and had counseled many people through their grief processes during that time. I scanned the shelves again, searching for a book a friend wrote about her grief process called *The Colors of Goodbye*.[2] I couldn't find it and felt a small disappointment because I so desperately wanted to help this poor woman.

After I walked through the next aisle and still had no luck, Ryan asked if she wanted him to pray with her. She nodded, tears rolling down her cheeks as she stood very still.

As Ryan said amen, Dan looked up and blurted out, "There it is!"

"There's what?" I asked.

"The book you were looking for!" he replied.

I couldn't believe it. He was right. It was literally right in front of us, placed in the wrong aisle, out of alphabetical order, and in the completely wrong genre. It sat on a shelf, almost as if it was waiting for us to find it.

We all teared up. Whether it was a literal miracle or just a happy accident, the magnitude of the moment was felt by all of us.

Rose actually chuckled as she reached out and took the book in her hands. "I feel like God sees me. Meeting you all, holding this book, I feel for the first time he sees me," she said between laughs and sobs.

As we left the bookstore, I asked Ryan what prompted him to start the conversation with her. He said, "She was just standing in the grieving section, and my heart felt for her."

I know Rose's feeling when she said she felt lost; I'm sure you do too. Perhaps it's what led you to pick up this book. In fact, you may be in a bookstore yourself right now, standing in the grief section, overwhelmed and unsure where to start. Somehow, you have stumbled across this book, and I am incredibly glad you have.

As I've navigated my own journey with grief, two central questions have guided me: *Why do we do what we do?* and *What do we do when life does what it does?* In researching the first question, I began taking notes that eventually led to my book *The Thing Beneath the Thing: What's Hidden Inside (and What God Helps Us Do About It).* The second question has taken me a long time to unravel, and yet it was precisely the arduous process of going through my own grief that helped me write this book. What you hold in your hands is my best effort to discover what we do when life does what it does. Some of the stories in these pages happened recently and some happened a long time ago. This in and of itself is an example of the complex and concentric nature of grief.

I wrote *Grieve, Breathe, Receive* for many reasons. I needed to write it for myself—to honor my grief, name some of the pain, and share more of my story with the world, hoping it might help others heal. Some parts are specific to my journey: stories about wounds I've tended, lies I've wrestled to the ground, breakdowns, and breakthroughs. Other parts I wrote with you in mind. I know what it is like to be at the end of your rope. I know how it feels when it seems like everyone else's life keeps spinning while you're stuck in the quicksand of your sorrow. I know that sensation when you want to be well but don't know how to get there.

While there is no perfect way to go through a season of pain and the subsequent grief that follows, there are tools we can access to aid us on the journey. In the Christian tradition, the Holy Weekend represents the Friday Jesus was executed on the cross; Saturday is the day between the grave and the resurrection; and Sunday is the day of newfound hope. We can look at *Grieve, Breathe, Receive* (GBR) through a similar lens. In *Grieve*, on Friday, we face the shock that comes whenever we encounter loss, change, tragedy, and unexpected disruption. In *Breathe*—Saturday—there is space, a time to try and make sense of the readjustment, disorientation, and confusion. This requires slowness and patience as you find your way through the grief. In *Receive*, on Sunday, we learn what it means to experience surprise, to realize a fresh hope that enables us to begin again, to evolve, and to embrace the possibility that exists in our tomorrow. This is what I call the GBR Journey.

I hope you will feel less alone as we begin this journey together through these words. I hope you will feel seen by God and others in rich and profound ways in the midst of your ache. Whatever has brought you to this moment is the catalyst for your healing as you find your way through your grief. Perhaps it was the loss of a loved one or the end of a relationship. Maybe it was the death of a dream that brought you to this book, or the shock of a diagnosis you didn't see coming. You may be here because you're exhausted by chronic pain or mental health struggles. You might not even be able to name the why (and that's more than OK!).

We don't need to qualify or justify our grief. We need to honor that we're here. And I want you to know that the pain that appeared unexpectedly on the doorstep of your life, whatever it might be, is not the end of your story. Your grief does not define you, although it does help shape you. As my wife, Sarah, says, "Your feelings matter, and they are not the most interesting thing about you." There is life after grief.

You are not lost, my friend. You are simply on your journey. I am honored to have this opportunity to walk this path with you. May these words help guide you on your quest for healing and renewal.

Grace + Peace,
Steve Carter

CHANGE

Honoring what comes up when change shows up

PART 1

GRIEVE

Welcome to *Friday*.

So, friends, what do we actually do when change arrives in our lives? Change is the result of adapting and responding to what comes our way, and it is an unavoidable part of life. Without change, we stagnate, we stall, we sink. Be that as it may, knowing change is necessary doesn't make it any easier to accept. Why? Because change often travels with grief. We can think of them as two sides of the same coin, joining us on our journey through life.

In order for change to make room for the future, something from our past must be set aside or adapted. This invokes a loss, a giving up of something. Grief fills the vacuum change creates when it visits. When you experience a change in your life, you can be sure that a wave of grief will follow. It's impossible to avoid the grief that change precedes, but we can learn to walk alongside it. The journey ahead may still be wrought with moments of pain, sadness, loneliness, and emptiness; however, as we go through this process we learn that those feelings serve as a reminder that as we are changing, we are also living. When you're ready, let's take a deep breath and step forward on our GBR Journey into the land of *Grieve*.

THE GRIEF JOURNEY

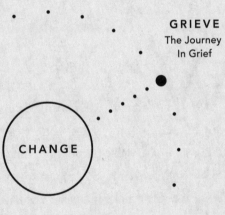

GRIEVE
The Journey
In Grief

CHANGE

CHAPTER 1

1,862 DAYS

What Do You Do When Life Does What It Does?

Life has a way of surprising us. And honestly, sometimes life makes zero sense.

You think it's going one way, but instead of going right, life dodges left. Or the rug gets pulled out from under you, leaving you leveled flat on the floor. For one reason, or maybe a hundred reasons, your life might not be like you thought it would right now, and the expectation for what this stage of life would be like is far from the reality of what it is.

So what do you do when life does what it does?

How do you cope when things don't go the way you expected?

A friend once told me that the hardest few years in a person's life are often thirty-eight to forty-three. When I pushed him for the reasoning behind this declaration, he said, "It's the ending of the first half of life and the beginning of the second half." As he spoke, I reflected on how accurate that statement felt to me. It definitely feels like a time in life when one has to wrestle with the reality that they're not as far along as they thought they would be financially, professionally, or relationally. This time isn't great for the ego because the body is changing, the motivation to achieve and succeed isn't as aggressive as it once was, and the energy is dwindling. Often, this is an age when many lose a parent, marriages end, and one must decide what they will leave behind to enter the second half well.

That conversation happened a few weeks before I turned thirty-eight. As my birthday approached, I couldn't shake the haunting thought that the hardest few years in a person's life are thirty-eight to forty-three. I remember thinking, *Don't speak that voodoo over me!*

One night, I woke up at 3:00 a.m. in a panic. I knew no one could predict the future, but something about my friend's words felt true. I grabbed my journal and did some simple math in a desperate attempt to figure out how many days I'd have to survive before I made it to the other side of those "danger years."

365 x 5 + 1 day for leap year.

1,826 days.

That's not that many days.

Honestly, what could go so wrong?

Maybe I could be like the 2016 Chicago Cubs when they broke the 108-year curse—perhaps I could get through these 1,826 days unscathed.

Famous. Last. Words.

At that time, my whole life felt like God had prepared me for the moment. All my effort, hard work, and striving were finally about to pay off in a culmination of timing. I was in the final stages of a five-year process for my dream job, and on the weekend of my thirty-eighth birthday, I was about to be named one of the successors. It all felt so surreal that a kid from Camarillo, California, with my background, would get the chance and opportunity to see his career dreams come true.

I felt like I had it all. I was married to an incredible woman, we had the two best kids on the planet, and we lived in a fantastic neighborhood in a house we adored that sat just down the street from some of our best friends. I had the chance to travel worldwide, meet incredible people, and serve in partnership with nonprofits dedicated to improving the world. I was speaking weekly to a congregation of over twenty-five thousand people. I was writing books I believed in and creating a sports podcast that was so much fun to make. And on occasion, I got to lead Bible studies for the Chicago Bears, a childhood dream fulfilled.

My life was extraordinary. It was honestly better than I could have ever imagined possible. It was . . . until it wasn't.

About three months after turning thirty-eight, everything

changed. The wheels began to fall off when multiple docu-
mented reports of sexual misconduct surfaced against Bill
Hybels, the founder of Willow Creek Community Church,
the church I was about to start leading. It shocked most of us
who worked, attended, and served at the church. For a while,
the message centered on getting to the bottom of things, and
some leaders suggested an investigation.

However, as I learned more, I discovered that some on
the elder board and one executive staff member had secretly
managed the victims, keeping their stories hidden for years.
The leadership landscape had crumbled, and as they tried to
hold on harder to their lies, the possibility of salvaging any
semblance of an honest future became hopeless. The betrayal
of trust and integrity was too much for me, and staying in that
role became impossible.

I was crushed. It was the death of a dream, sure, but also
a shattering of the image I held of my mentor, whom I'd
always respected and now knew had harbored lies and abuse
for years. I couldn't stomach the tragic ways so many women's
lives had been forever altered and wounded due to his neglect
of their boundaries and safety. Just before turning thirty-nine,
I resigned in protest of the church leaders' decision to protect
the abuser and the institution instead of the victims who had
come forward.

The fallout over my decision was immediate and catastrophic. Longtime friends felt betrayed by my decision to
resign and were divided on which side to choose: the abused
women or the church. The choice was clear to me and left us

at an impasse. My social media became a hot spot for angry comments and threatening messages. My family could barely leave the house as news spread across the globe and press trucks showed up in our yard.

I wasn't even halfway through that five-year window my friend had warned me about, and it was already too much.

As I will share in more detail later, about five months after I resigned, we moved to Arizona to be near my wife's family and attempt to catch our breath and figure out what we would do next. I was keeping myself busy, too afraid to slow down and feel the deep grief the last few months had caused me. (It was not a great strategy, as I'm sure you can imagine.) And then, my adoptive father, whom I call Dad and who had raised me since I was two, passed away after complications with leukemia. The man who meant everything to me was gone, and I couldn't fix it.

The ache of grief was growing louder and louder, but I kept covering my ears and powering through, trying my best to escape my pain.

And then, in another heartbreaking loss that I'll unfold later, I learned the story I'd been told all my life about why my biological father had left me when I was young wasn't the whole story. The man I thought had bailed on me and saddled me with a lifetime of abandonment fears had been trying to find me for years. But I couldn't contact him now because he had also passed away years before. Imagine trying to save a sinking ship by bailing water with an eyedropper. That was how ridiculous my meager attempts to keep grief at bay were then.

There was no escaping my grief. It was more than my heart and mind could handle. The darkness of loss became a heavy blanket covering my days. I could barely leave my bed, willing myself to get up only because I knew I had to show up and work or we couldn't afford rent or groceries. I struggled to find hope and went on medication to help me cope.

I dove deep into therapy and had to confront a few harsh realities I'd been avoiding. For the first half of my life, I had been working to achieve success to be loved enough, safe enough, and secure enough. That motivation slowly morphed into my identity and became my justification for workaholism. I lost years of memories and chances for attachment by avoiding connection and throwing myself into work environments where I could ride the dopamine high of success. My wife and kids paid dearly for my addiction.

Just over a year after we moved to the desert, the world slowed to a crawl as COVID-19 took over communities. Millions of lives were lost, and every inch of humanity felt the collective grief of an entire planet. Schools and businesses closed their doors, and most ways we worked and lived became virtual. Those who stayed in physical jobs became heroes: our postal workers, grocers, nurses, doctors, and countless others who took on nearly impossible tasks to keep us fed, connected, and protected.

Our kids, Emerson and Mercy, had only just started making new friends when they were moved to virtual learning at home, another blow for their already fragile hearts.

Strangely, being forced to slow down and stay home was

central to my reconciliation with grief. I could not run away from it. I had to remain in my small world, isolated with my family and without accolades to help take the edge off my sadness. I had to learn how to make friends with my grief in order to survive. Throughout the pandemic, I slowly began to understand that grief was a friend rather than a foe. A phrase lingered in my mind that gradually became an anchoring guide as I learned to embrace, rather than fear, grief.

Grieve. Breathe. Receive.

Little did I know then how those three words would start to form and shape a life-changing anthem for me as I allowed God to break down my understanding of each of them and reform their meanings and myself into something new during the next several years. I've immersed myself in research on a quest for understanding, which launched from my encounters with pain and loss.

Over time, I've collected stories and wisdom from mentors, therapists, spiritual directors, ancient wisdom traditions, and some unexpected practices that have helped me learn to work with my grief rather than against it. How do we do this?

We begin this work by honoring what comes up when change shows up.

Novelist Octavia Butler wrote, "All that you touch, you change. All that you change changes you. The only lasting truth is change. God is change."[1] That struck me.

The only lasting truth is change. Those of us who have experienced loss know how true this is. Especially when confronted with grief, having the knowledge and courage to face this change will alter us forever. We have a choice as we start to acknowledge the parts of our story that have been painful, sad, disappointing, unexpected, and full of loss. We can try suppressing those more challenging emotions that come when grieving. We can distract ourselves from grief by increasing our life's volume, staying busy, professionally challenged, or keeping our social calendars and credit cards maxed out. Or we can try befriending our grief. We can get curious and courageous, letting go of the tricks that keep us running from sadness and instead making room for what it may want to show us about ourselves and the world.

What you are holding in your hands is my best attempt to help you rediscover hope after the unexpected and unthinkable happens. These three words—*grieve, breathe, receive*—became a mantra, a torch I carried through the most brutal season of my life that allowed me to discover, uncover, and recover all that had been taken from me. I pray these words will give you help and hope so that you can successfully and courageously discover a way through all the changes this life will eventually bring.

Who are you in the face of change? Are you ready to find out?

Reflection Questions

1. Take a moment to reflect on the question asked at the end of this chapter: Who are you in the face of change? What comes to your mind? Write it down so you can return to it throughout this GBR Journey.
2. What do you usually do when encountering something sad, painful, or disappointing? Why do you think that is?
3. What change are you struggling to honor right now?

CHAPTER 2

BORN IDENTITY

Who Do You Say That I Am?

I was given the name Stephen Charles Born at birth. Charles was my father's name (though he went by Chuck). Before my earliest memory formed, my parents split up. I don't remember meeting or knowing Chuck. All I had of him were a handful of negative stories and a shoebox filled with photos and mementos: an old military photograph that strongly resembled me, an old driver's license with his name and photo, a few birthday cards he sent me, and some newspaper clippings of my multi-star-general grandfather. Sometimes I would pull out that box and look through the items within, but I didn't fully understand how they were related to my past.

After my mom remarried and Joel adopted me, I stopped opening the box altogether. No one asked me to do that. I suppose it felt like a violation to yearn for a father I was told didn't want me when I now had a perfectly good new dad in Joel. The shoebox and its proof of Chuck sat collecting dust under my twin bed for years. As I got a little older, I started to think more about Chuck, curiosity brimming as I became more self-aware. Joel had a temper, and on his bad days, I'd go to my room, pull out that box, and imagine life with Chuck.

The framing narrative I had been handed was that Chuck left because he didn't want to be a dad, but it was a good thing because he wasn't a good role model for me anyway. Being so young, I internalized this narrative and turned it toward me: *I must be the reason Chuck left. There must be something wrong with me.* Maybe I was unlovable or not worth sticking around for. For much of my early years into adulthood, I struggled to believe I was good enough for anyone to love me. Kids are very perceptive about the world but are often bad interpreters of its reality.

What we perceive and the stories we create, believe, and embody are where things can go astray quite quickly. I perceived that Chuck had abandoned me, and I carried with me an interpretation that he left because I hadn't been enough for him to stick around for. My remedy for that was to focus on being the best. I was terrified of failing and suffered from anxiety, feeling the weight of the other relationships in my life resting squarely on my ability to perform.

After Sarah and I returned from our honeymoon, we learned my parents had separated on our wedding day, and shortly thereafter, they divorced. Their divorce revived my long-buried desire to find Chuck. It felt less like a betrayal of my adoptive dad now that my mom and Joel weren't married, and I had some lingering questions I wanted answered that neither he nor my mom were providing. I discovered that Chuck had been living in upstate New York. I decided to travel there and see if I could find a way to get in touch with him (this was before the wonders of Google were widely accessible). Sarah and my mom chose to join me on the trip. I grew increasingly nervous as the travel date drew closer. *Am I really ready to meet him? How will it feel to see him face-to-face for the first time? Will I be angry? Will I cry?* I tried to picture the moment but couldn't get my head around it.

A few days before our departure, I discovered Chuck had passed away two years earlier, and the address hadn't been updated from his name in the public record. It was a devastating blow to the reunion I'd imagined in my head. I could already tell my grief at this lost opportunity would be with me for a long time. I decided I still wanted to go on the trip. If nothing else, I hoped to find the place where Chuck was buried to have a chance to get some closure. I was also curious about the house being in his name—did that mean he had relatives still living there? If so, who would they be to me? Just the thought of it sent my mind spinning.

When we arrived at the house, no one was home. I felt defeated but still hopeful for a way to find his gravesite. I was grasping for something I could point to that would make the trip out there feel worth it.

We tracked down the cemetery where he was buried and drove there on a gray and chilly fall morning. There wasn't anyone nearby, the intermittent rain perhaps keeping away most visitors for the day. We split up, reading the carved letters of hundreds of moss-covered headstones, before I read the words I'd been looking for: *Charles Franklin Born.*

I met my biological father in a small cemetery in Afton, New York.

I dropped to my knees and wept. I wept for the loss, not only of his life but of time, relationship, and the chance to have known each other. I didn't know anything about him, but his gravestone had a spiritual quote, and I wondered if he'd been religious. Had he found God, maybe peace, and a happy life? I wished I'd had the chance to know him. I was left alone, with a head filled with questions and no way to get answers.

Have you ever experienced the kind of surprise that you never saw coming? I'm talking about an earth-shattering, identity-shaking kind of surprise. Sometimes these surprises can be good, like finding out you're pregnant after trying to have a baby for a while, or learning that you got into your dream college. And sometimes they are not so good, like discovering an affair or receiving a difficult medical report. And sometimes, they are both good and bad, hard and beautiful.

About ten years ago, I experienced a surprise like that when I received the most unexpected email: "My name is Kathy Born. I was married to your father, Chuck. Recently, I came across one of your teachings, and it startled me how much you sounded and looked like your dad. I'd love to share if you are ever open to connecting and learning more about Chuck."

It was the ultimate "I did not see this coming" moment.

I stared at the screen, feeling a mix of fear, shock, and excitement. I'd given up on ever having the chance to learn more about my biological father, and now, when I least expected it, I'd been given an invitation. I couldn't get over her words that I sounded and looked like my dad. I had no idea what his voice was like. I don't have a single memory of him, and somehow hearing this broke me. I knew then I wanted to know more. I wanted to hear as much as she was up for telling me about Chuck.

I crafted an email back to her, thanking her for reaching out and including a few questions about Chuck I was really curious about.

"What was he like?"

"Was he a man of faith?"

"How did he die?"

"Did he ever think of me?"

"Did he follow along with my life from afar?"

"Did he ever tell you why he left me?"

She graciously wrote back, answering my questions and telling me he had a picture of me on his nightstand. She said her grown daughter had come across me on her social media and sent her a video of one of my teachings.

I was struggling to catch up. My mind was stuck on the first thing she'd told me. He had a photo of me on his night-stand. How could that be? Why would a guy who didn't want to be my dad keep a photo so close?

Our correspondence continued, and she offered more details as I asked more questions. "Chuck never left you, Steve. There is a lot you don't know."

To be honest, I didn't want to know what she meant by it, although something deep within rang true, and I knew that when I started to pull that thread, a crucial piece of my past would unravel.

Kathy and I continued to email and talk on the phone over the following years, but we hadn't yet met in person. As I entered my desert season of grief, I knew I needed to know more about what Kathy had shared with me.

I booked a flight and flew to Providence, Rhode Island, and we met for a meal.

Kathy told me that all those years ago, when Chuck signed away his rights to me, he was told that he was signing papers that gave up his obligation to pay child support. He had no idea he was relinquishing his parental rights to me. My heart broke as I imagined how he must have felt when reality sank in. I found out that when I was four years old, Chuck and Kathy had come to pick me up from my house for Christmas, and no one answered the door. When they couldn't reach my mom, they asked a neighbor where we'd gone.

"They moved to Michigan," the neighbor informed them.

At that moment, I had a flashback to playing in the snow in Michigan when I was little. Could that have been the same moment my dad realized he'd lost me forever?

Kathy continued, "There were no cell phones or internet. We had no idea where you were. We learned that you lived in California when you were eight or nine. As much as Chuck longed to travel to see you, he feared that too much time had passed, and you wouldn't know who he was. He didn't want to disrupt your life any more than it already had been. But he always wished to have a relationship with you."

I shook my head, trying hard to find a way to make it all make sense. I thought he left me. Didn't he abandon me? All this time, I'd thought he bailed.

After meeting with Kathy, I felt oddly comforted yet deeply disturbed by what I'd uncovered. Instead of returning home, I changed my flight to Grand Rapids, where Joel lived. I had to know if he knew about all this. More than anything, I needed to look him in the eye when I asked him to tell me the truth.

When I arrived at Joel's house, we hugged, and he could see immediately that I wasn't OK. We made our way to his living room, and he slowly sat in his favorite chair, oxygen tubes in both nostrils, the machine humming beside him. As I spoke, his eyes filled with tears, and he struggled to meet mine. He shook his head and whispered, "I'm so sorry, bud."

It was true. Chuck didn't leave me. He was forced out of my life. I could barely breathe.

Joel told me he'd been told a similar story to the one I'd grown up with. Chuck was a bad guy, a deadbeat dad, an addict who would cause me more pain than he was worth. Joel had believed it all, and why wouldn't he? Neither of us had any reason to suspect different back then.

The untangling of this old story was overwhelming for the next few months. I continued to grieve and follow the GBR Journey: honor the change that had come up while trying hard to stay present to the pain that had been stirred up. This was a change I hadn't seen coming. So much of my story of origin was a lie. So much of who I am was built on a false narrative.

A couple of years later while I was hiking a mountain trail in Arizona called Tom's Thumb, a profound realization hit me: *What happened with Chuck is what happened with Willow.*

Regarding both my biological father and my church home, I had believed in a lie and built a future on that lie. I had let someone else tell me a story and then used it as a frame for my life. But the story was not true, and I was left holding the bag.

When I was at Willow, the founding pastor would suggest that I wasn't a good leader. I heard that I was a teacher but I didn't have it in me to lead. The words *you couldn't lead yourself out of a paper bag* float through my mind. By all accounts, he was a leader. He led the Global Leadership Summit and was an internationally respected leader, so who was I to question him? I didn't question a thing. I let his words cut and sink in deep, believing what he said was true about me. Now that I have some perspective, it's easier to see that I was being manipulated. But back then, I was too close to separate truth from lies. Which made me wonder: What else had I so easily believed?

I wonder if you can relate. I know many of us have experienced manipulation, gaslighting, and other forms of abuse designed to control us. Those who've experienced infidelity know this well too. When we realize we've been tricked, managed, and controlled by someone else's lies, it becomes hard to look back and differentiate the truth from the rest.

This happened more than I cared to admit at Willow.

Once, I had invited a highly respected business leader to speak at a small leadership event at the church. Unexpectedly, the turnout was amazing, and almost a thousand people showed up. In my mind, it was a huge success. I was excited to debrief the event with the founder, who was traveling in another part of the world. In an email, I told him how well it had gone, reporting the numbers, the feedback, and some of the connections created.

I'll never forget his response: "That's not what I heard."

Which led me to write back, "What did you hear?"

He berated me, asking me what I was thinking in bringing the speaker there and claiming that because he didn't share the gospel, it was a mistake that didn't serve our church. And then, for the kicker, he told me he was beginning to lose trust in my ability to discern Willow's culture. He told me that in the future I would need to run every decision I made by him.

I was shocked because his reaction was so far off my expectation radar that I couldn't understand it. The math didn't make sense. Everyone I'd asked about it had loved the event, and given the turnout, I was certain the speaker had been a smart choice to inspire Willow's leaders.

Still, rather than question him, I accepted his judgment. I went on to feel shame and embarrassment for years, thinking I had royally screwed up.

Later—in the spring of 2018—when the founder and our leadership team learned the *Chicago Tribune* was investigating reports of sexual misconduct and abuse of power by our founder,[1] I was called into a meeting with elders, staff members, and two public relations firms. You read that right. There were *two* PR firms present at that meeting. I had no clue what I'd walked into. The PR representative was peppering two elders with hypothetical questions to essentially "practice" their responses to questions the journalists might ask during the interview. At one point, she asked them how they would respond regarding the naked woman on the boat.

I raised my hand, flabbergasted. "Excuse me, what naked woman on a boat? Is this a story that really happened? Can someone please explain this to me?"

The *Tribune* story mentioned the woman who was seen swimming naked. The story the elders then told was shocking: the husband of this woman had sent the founder a letter telling him that if he ever talked to his wife again, he would "kick his ass." Unknowingly, I'd asked this man to speak at our church after this. Well, now the founder's reaction made more sense. Maybe it hadn't been about me in the first place, but rather the perceived risk and potential catastrophe he had been hiding.

At the end of the day, this is a conversation about identity. I remember hearing speaker Christine Caine teach this concept when discussing a passage in Genesis 3 when she spoke at Willow years back.[2] After Adam and Eve hid from God because they were naked, God asked them, "Who told you?" (v. 11). *Who told you this about yourself?*

As I considered my life story up to that point, I began asking myself questions about certain moments.

When Chuck left me, I was told he didn't want me. *Who told you?*

When I brought that guest speaker to Willow, I was told I was a bad leader. *Who told you?*

When I later stood up for the victims and resigned, I was told I was a selfish coward. *Who told you?*

As we begin to ask ourselves those questions, we must be prepared to make room for the answers. We encounter grief as we look back with compassion at our past selves and observe how we were manipulated by people we trusted. Maybe some specific memories or words come to mind as you read this. I'd invite you to take the time to ask yourself these questions:

Who told you that?
Do you agree or disagree with them?
What do you believe is true now?

I never knew my biological dad, and that was not my fault.
I am a leader, and I was not the problem.
I am an ally, and I did what was right.

You are not what happened to you; you can decide your true self. This doesn't absolve us from our responsibility to grow, but it does set boundaries on what is ours to hold and what is not. As we reclaim what is true, we recalibrate and have a chance to change how our future will unfold.

Reflection Questions

1. What story comes to mind from your own life when you read this chapter? What similarities and differences do you notice?

2. Are there negative or harmful things you have accepted as true about yourself that have been handed to you by someone else? Take a moment to reflect and write them down. Then, write a counterstatement that is true about yourself now. What old stories do you need to let go of so that you can move forward on this GBR Journey?

CHAPTER 3

THE QUESTION

Did You Have Integrity Today?

I pulled the car over on a dusty back road between Chicago, Illinois, and Madison, Wisconsin, in the heat of late summer. I felt shaky and alert, as if the adrenaline coursing through my veins would set me on fire. My wife, Sarah, stepped out of the car while I called Joel and told him I was resigning from my dream job. Even as I uttered the words on the phone, I cried. I felt out of my body, as if I were suddenly living someone else's life—I couldn't seem to get my bearings. My dad gently responded, "It's the right move, and I'm so sorry, son. I've never been prouder of you.

It's going to be all right." His words broke the dam, and my tears fell heavily.

I hung up and watched my wife walk back toward the car; both of our kids were still asleep in the back seat. I told her what my dad said, my voice trailing and unable to finish my sentence. *How did it come to this?* I sighed heavily as we uploaded my resignation letter onto my blog. I said a prayer internally and then pressed Publish.

Immediately after my resignation went live online, I doubled over, falling into Sarah's arms, overcome with grief. This was the only way we could do it, and we both knew it. We had tried to trust the church leadership to handle my resignation process, only to have them manage, delay, and manipulate it. No, I needed this to be public and immediate in order to maintain integrity and support the victims, even if it broke my heart.

I took a deep breath, turned off my phone, and pulled back onto the highway toward Madison.

■

What a devastating few hours it had been.

Just before sunrise on that gray Sunday morning, my phone began vibrating as multiple texts poured in. I quickly opened the home screen to at least twenty different friends who had sent me the same *New York Times* article titled "He's a Superstar Pastor. She Worked for Him and Said He Groped Her Repeatedly."[1]

Hybels had been my mentor and boss for several years. He'd been someone I'd deeply admired until I learned of the several allegations of sexual abuse and abuse of power against him. I and the world had read about these allegations as reported by multiple former staff and spouses spanning decades, but as I'd come to find out, behind secret doors, the elder board and one other executive staff person had known about these misconduct allegations for years.

Starting from the top, I read and reread the article filled with horrifying stories of sexual misconduct and accounts of power and spiritual abuse committed by Hybels against his former assistant, Ms. Baranowski, including photos of handwritten notes he had sent her while she was his assistant that crossed lines of sexual harassment. It was sick. Gut-wrenching. Horrific on every level.

Deep sadness and profound anger were fighting internally for control of my body as I attempted to process what I was reading and what would happen next. Indeed, this changed everything, even for the elders and executive staff who, up until this point, had not said Bill had committed any sin.

I willed myself to get out of bed and shower. I wasn't sure what to expect when I arrived at Willow. Still, I hoped the executive staff would outline a plan to address these grave allegations in a pastoral manner in the emergency leadership team meeting they called before services began. Someone from each church campus was represented in person or by conference phone as the lead executive pastor presented her plan not to address the *New York Times* article or mention Bill Hybels from the stage.

I took a deep breath and pulled up my chair, clearing my burning throat as I began to speak. I told the team we had to address the article and all it presented. I urged them to take it seriously, to use this opportunity to admit openly what Bill had done and publicly invite him to repent. I reminded them that this was bigger than Willow, that even as we sat there, the *New York Times* article was being retweeted again and again globally. Not only did our congregation need to hear from their pastors, but the entire global church did too.

I was shut down and told the topic would still not be addressed in service. It felt as if the walls were closing in and all the air was being sucked out of the room. I suddenly felt dizzy and faint. I excused myself as I raced to the small back restroom and vomited, my body unable to hold all the sickness I felt within.

As I washed my face, I pictured my son, Emerson, and remembered what my high school pastor, a lanky revolutionary named Hal, used to tell me: "I don't care how many points you score in a game. I don't care where you go to college or what you do for a living. I only care if you aim to have integrity every day. Integrity takes seconds, minutes, hours, days, weeks, months, years, and decades to build and mere seconds to lose. So here's the question, Steve: Did you have integrity today?"

It's a question I'd often recite with my son before bed. Even when Emerson was a newborn swaddled up in his crib, I'd move my face close to his perfect head and whisper, "I love you, bud, and I hope I'll always make you proud and practice integrity every day as your dad."

When he was old enough to talk, he'd ask, "Dada, what does *integrity* mean?" I'd simply say, "Integrity is when you say what you mean, mean what you say, and live by its creed no matter what."

Then I'd ask him, "So, bud, did you have integrity today?"

He'd say, "I think so! How about you, Dad?"

I'd reply, "I think so, kiddo." Then I'd kiss his forehead as he snuggled in and fell asleep.

I was still standing in the cold bathroom, staring at the mirror, trying to discern what this moment asked of me. I remembered a night about seven weeks earlier when I'd met with the church elders and told them I believed the women. I had written an article I'd planned to post to my blog, but they were not pleased. It was a difficult conversation on many levels. It felt like the first time I was going against the grain and breaking from the company line.

When I'd left that meeting and headed home, all the lights were off. Sarah and the kids had gone to bed hours earlier. I quietly stepped from the garage to the kitchen and set down my phone. I was exhausted, my adrenals were shot, and cortisol pumped through my body as I decided to make myself a gin and tonic. As I cut up a lime, I heard footsteps on the hardwood floor coming down the hallway. I peeked around the corner and saw Emerson sleepily walk out.

He ran up and hugged me, then looked me in the eyes and asked, "Dad, did you have integrity today?"

I couldn't believe it. I began to tear up as I bent down on one knee and said, "I think so, bud. It was tough today, but I think I did."

He quickly responded, "I bet you did." Then he gave me another huge hug and went back to bed.

That moment was replaying as I walked back into the Sunday morning meeting. If I went along with their plan not to say a word about Bill, the *New York Times* article, or the gut-wrenching accounts of abuse outlined by his former assistant, how would I answer my son's question that night? If I just got onstage, pretended nothing had happened, and went about my interview with NPR's Ira Glass as intended that morning, I knew I would betray my integrity. I winced as I realized this, knowing I'd have to look my son in the eye as I admitted that I hadn't.

I looked around the table at the people gathered, busy plotting ways to manage and survive the article and all its damning evidence, and felt the words rising within: *Say what you mean, mean what you say, and live out its creed no matter what.*

I felt sick again and knew I needed to get out of there. I told the team my stomach was a wreck, and I could not go onstage. I stumbled to my car and drove home before the morning services began. I walked straight into my bedroom and pulled the covers over my head, feeling the weight of what I knew this decision would mean and initiate.

Sarah gave me time to process before she carefully came in and asked, "What will you do?"

I replied in a whisper, "I have to resign."

She nodded and dropped her hands to her side. It was as if life had been sucked from our lungs. I pulled out the laptop and began typing these words:

I am writing to announce my resignation from Willow Creek Community Church, effective immediately.

The new facts and allegations that came to light this morning are horrifying, and my heart goes out to Ms. Baranowski and her family for the pain they have lived with. These most recent revelations have also compelled me to make public my decision to leave, as much as it grieves me to go.

Since the first women came forward with their stories, I have been gravely concerned about our church's official response, and it's [sic] ongoing approach to these painful issues. After many frank conversations with our elders, it became clear that there is a fundamental difference in judgment between what I believe is necessary for Willow Creek to move in a positive direction, and what they think is best. That is not to say that I am right and they are wrong. But I must follow the path that I believe God has laid out for me to live with integrity, and that path now diverges from Willow Creek. I offered my resignation many weeks ago, but I was requested to delay an announcement and continue with my duties until the leadership determined how to make the decision public. At this point, however, I cannot, in good conscience, appear before you as your Lead Teaching Pastor when my soul is so at odds with the institution.

I wish I could appear before you to say goodbye. I wish I could tell each of you, personally and individually, how much I treasure the time I have been able to serve you. But it would be misleading of me to stand on that stage as if presenting a unified front. I defer to the wisdom of the leadership of this church, so I must stand aside.

Sarah and I are heartbroken over this decision. We love our Willow Creek family. Nothing would have given me more joy than to pastor this church for many years to come.

To all the congregants, staff, believers, supporters, and wonderfully faithful people who make up this community, thank you so much for the opportunity to be a part of your world. I thank God for every moment I've had with you here, and we will continue to pray for this community and hold it dearly in our hearts.

Grace + Peace,
Steve Carter[2]

We knew we couldn't post my resignation while we were still home because we'd already had multiple news crews staking out our house during the past few weeks. Sarah filled overnight bags for the kids and us while I tried to stave off a panic attack. We used up our travel points on a hotel in Madison, loaded bags and our family into our car, and headed north, pulling off on that dusty back road where I hit Publish.

■

As we drove into Madison, the rain was coming down, and the hotel we planned to stay at was oversold. We needed a room. We found another last-minute hotel and grabbed food in the restaurant next door. We were both comatose for most of the evening. Our phones were still turned off, and we had no idea what people were saying in response to my resignation. We didn't know how Willow had spun it or what they'd said about the *New York Times* article. I felt everything and nothing all at once.

I crashed and slept hard until 5:00 a.m. before it started to hit me. Fear and anxiety came over me as I scanned the still-dark hotel room. My kids were asleep in the other bed, their little faces looking so peaceful it made my heart ache. What would my decision mean for their lives?

My inner monologue wouldn't stop spiraling:

What have I done?

I don't have another job.

What am I going to do now?

How am I going to provide for my family?

I could see why so many people stayed silent when the

abuse happened. The cost was just too great. Relationally. Financially. Professionally.

I decided to try clearing my head by walking around downtown Madison. I loaded up my backpack with my Bible, journal, pen, and phone and left Sarah a note that I'd be back soon.

It was still early, and I noted how the darkness around me matched the swirling in my head. I turned my phone on for the first time since publishing my resignation post, and within seconds it lit up with notifications. Foolishly, I began to read them. Then I switched over to social media and opened some of the many messages that came in:

"You are a coward."

"You're a con man."

"You're a disappointment!"

"You do not deserve to be in ministry."

"You bailed."

"You're a joke."

"I never liked you anyway!"

"You abandoned us when we needed you most!"

"You're what's wrong with the church!"

"Shame on you, Steve Carter."

"I hate you!"

"You're a wolf in sheep's clothing!"

"You're the worst &^£%+@¥ pastor ever!"

I'd never experienced that level of public ridicule before. There were the usual trolls, but many of these comments were posted by people I knew and loved. The weight of their words hit like a mallet, and suddenly I couldn't breathe again.

I made it about a block before I crumbled on the sidewalk, weeping as the weight of what just happened sank in.

Overwhelmed.

Exhausted.

Sad.

Angry.

Scared.

I looked up to the heavens and begged desperately, *I need a word, Lord, please. Can you give me anything to let me know we're gonna be all right?*

I waited and heard nothing but the heavy traffic coming down the road. I walked a few more blocks before sitting on a bench across from the capitol building. I watched people come and go for a while. I unzipped my backpack and grabbed my Bible and journal. I opened my journal to the first page and scanned the Cadet Prayer, sacred words I've carried with me over the years:

Strengthen and increase our admiration for honest dealing and clean thinking, and suffer not our hatred of hypocrisy and pretense ever to diminish. Encourage us in our endeavor to live above the common level of life. Make us choose the harder right instead of the easier wrong, and never to be content with a half truth when the whole can be won.

Endow us with courage that is born of loyalty to all that is noble and worthy, that scorns to compromise with vice and injustice and knows no fear when truth and right are in jeopardy.

Guard us against flippancy and irreverence in the sacred things of life. Grant us new ties of friendship and new opportunities of service. Kindle our hearts in fellowship with those of a cheerful countenance, and soften our hearts with sympathy for those who sorrow and suffer.[3]

I read the prayer.

I reread the prayer.

It didn't seem to calm my spirit, but the angst of what felt like injustice started to boil. Internally, I screamed, *I thought this is what I did, Lord!*

I chose the more complex right instead of the easier wrong. I was not content with the institution's half-truths, and I did what I could to honor the women who reported their abuse. I stood up for what was right. So why was I feeling all this angst if I actually did the right thing?

Still nothing from God.

I cried out, *Please give me something. Please!*

The words *grieve, breathe,* and *receive* rose to my consciousness from somewhere deep within. I didn't know what the words meant in relation to my circumstances, but I knew how they felt in my spirit. Wiping my tears, I exhaled and had a sense of hope. The fog began to lift. In a moment of sheer desperation, I started to see a map develop that would become a guide for me in the journey:

- **GRIEVE** what is, grieve what I thought it would be, and grieve how key people let me down.
- **BREATHE** in goodness, peace, and mercy, and exhale all the bitterness, resentment, and anger.
- **RECEIVE** what I need to learn, what I need to own, and who I will become.

I had a solid sense of a path forward. It wasn't clear, but it was a start to keep me moving. I flipped the page and wrote out a personal commitment.

Starting right now, my sole focus will be to:

1. grieve, breathe, receive
2. help my family heal well, and
3. still create beautiful things.

These were the three goals on my list, and they were a precious reminder that I wasn't alone or without purpose. What I thought was the end of my life would become my story of origin. The same is true for you.

Friends, as much as we want to control our circumstances, especially when we're in the midst of disruption or loss, the truth is that we just can't. It can feel too overwhelming, too impossible to face the enormity of our grief all at once. One of the ways we can approach this is by keeping it small and focusing on something we can commit to right now. This could be a daily mantra, a list, charting goals, or prayer. The most important thing is that you are consistently showing up

GRIEVE BREATHE RECEIVE

to this practice by staying focused on small, actionable steps. This framework can help you take brave ground in your GBR Journey.

Reflection Questions

1. What is a moment in your own life when you had to make a difficult decision? Is there anything you would change or do differently now?
2. How does Steve's story of loss connect to your grief? Where in his story can you find yourself?
3. In what ways are you practicing integrity in your daily life?

CHAPTER 4

SUBMARINE

Is There Any Hope?

About a week before Christmas in 1927, a navy submarine and a coast guard ship collided in the Atlantic Ocean a mile off the coast of Provincetown, Massachusetts. How could this have happened? What are the odds of two ships accidentally crashing into each other in an ocean three thousand miles wide, spanning 20 percent of the earth's surface, and covering roughly forty-one million square miles?

The loss was significant for the crew of the USS *S-4* submarine. The team took on water and began to sink seventeen fathoms deep (about 106 feet). The six crew members who were still alive locked themselves in the hull, waiting and praying to be rescued.

The US Coast Guard and US Navy went into emergency mode. They sent divers down to explore the damage and heard loud tapping from within. The crew was trying to communicate in Morse code. Through the deep water came a metal tinging:

I-S—T-H-E-R-E—A-N-Y—H-O-P-E?

I can't imagine having been one of those divers hearing that desperate question. It's a question we all ask as we navigate loss, isn't it? When we face an outcome we cannot control and wish we could change, our pain and disappointment lurking underneath the surface collide with the persona of control we maintain above the surface, leaving massive collateral damage we must deal with. The reality is, the majority of the process of healing after loss is hard, thankless work. There are usually many moments as we move through the experience of grief when we stop and ask the same question: *Is there any hope?*

There is more to life than just pain and sorrow, and thank God for that, but for most of us, it's challenging to know what to do when life gets painful. What do we do when life brings us

Loss?
Death?
Betrayal?
Divorce?
Unmet expectations?

Relationships fractured?

Disappointment?

Dreams shattered?

Injustice?

Abuse?

Disease?

Collateral damage?

Hurts?

Pain?

Change?

One afternoon, I was beginning to process my grief with a mentor after leaving Willow when he said something that shocked me: "Grieve often, feel it all; but whatever you do, please don't grieve without hope."

Grief and hope. Pairing those together felt like an oxymoron, like unlikely dance partners destined to get the choreography wrong. My understanding of hope at that time was based more on whimsy and platitudes than anything profound and biblical.

His comment struck a chord with me, and I spent several weeks researching everything I could find to help expand my understanding of hope.

As a pastor with an affinity for history, I dug into the Scriptures and talked to a few mentors to see how hope was perceived and lived out in past generations. One of those conversations was with John Ortberg. He helped me understand hope and the ancient Roman world in an entirely new way.

He began describing for me how in the first century, people didn't hold hope in high regard. People thought so little of it that they ridiculed others for demonstrating any semblance of hope. Roman culture was at the center of this. In grammar school, they had kids try to limit dreaming and hoping by creating what is commonly referred to as a "hardship list," where they would predict trials, tribulations, and suffering they could encounter in the future and write them down. Can you imagine how traumatic that would be today if third graders had to journal their most scary and catastrophic fears, writing them down as if they were guaranteed to happen someday?

The Romans wanted their kids to be prepared to handle the situations of hardship they knew would be part of their future. To make it in their world, you had to withstand the suffering. Emotion and sensitivity were liabilities to avoid, while reason and logic were tools for survival in Rome. If you had hope, you ran the risk of being considered weak, because some in the ancient world believed hope to be like a moral disease (a sign of weakness). It meant you depended on a power outside yourself.

In our modern American world, hope has been trivialized and tamed, something we stick on key chains and bumper stickers and weave onto throw pillows. We toss the word around carelessly, making offhand comments like, "I hope the Chicago Cubs win the World Series" or "I hope there is no traffic on the highway."

There is nothing wrong with using hope this way. I do it, too, especially when I'm running late and need all the lights to be green on my route to my office! My alma mater is called Hope International. Once I heard that they got their name because when deciding what to call the college, they put *hope* as a placeholder, as in, "We hope we can decide on a name soon!" After a while, the name stuck, and they decided it was the perfect name for what they wanted: to instill hope in their students. Talk about a far cry from the Romans, right?

However, that type of hope and the more trivial kind are wildly different from what I'm talking about when I refer to the type of hope related to the grief process. The hope we're after now is a gritty and courageous hope, the kind we find when we've run out of platitudes and niceties. Hebrews 6:11–12 states, "And we desire that each one of you demonstrate the same diligence so as to realize the full assurance of hope until the end, so that you will not be sluggish, but imitators of those who through faith and endurance inherit the promises" (NASB).

Notice the words the writer chose to use in this text: *the full assurance of hope*. The total confidence—not flippant wishing in uncertainty, not throwing words around to make ourselves feel better, but a complete hope.

During my quest to understand the relationship between grief and hope, I spoke with a friend who gave me a challenge. After discussing the merits of what makes hope complete, he said, "Carter, I dare you to hope."

My kids and I often play truth or dare when bored. Most of the time, we choose "dare" because we love to try to make one another laugh, whether singing loudly to Taylor Swift in the grocery store or dancing wildly in front of the school at morning drop-off. On the rare occasion when someone chooses "truth," we learn more about them, and it turns into a sweet and insightful conversation.

But being dared to hope was new to me.

I'd never considered hope dangerous, so my friend's phrasing surprised me. What's so scary about hope, anyway? As I sat with my friend's challenge to me, I realized there was some fear bubbling up inside, tiny sparks of anxiety starting to stir as I considered the weight of choosing to hope.

What if I get my hopes up too much?
What if I get let down?
What if I try to hope, but it remains elusive?

Remember those six crew members on the submarine who found themselves trapped? We left them as they'd tapped out their question: "Is there any hope?" but the truth is, despite the US Navy's best efforts, they could not rescue those men in time. Sometimes we choose to hope and get what we wish for. Sometimes we choose to hope, and we don't. Regardless, I have to imagine the fact that those men spent their final hours with hope in their hearts made their passing more peaceful than if they had lost all hope.

The truth is, just because we hope for something doesn't mean we'll get it. Hope is risky. Wanting is vulnerable.

So how do we work through the risks and learn to use hope as an ally and an opportunity to move through our grief? Honestly, we start by saying what we want out loud to ourselves or a trusted friend, partner, or therapist, or in a journal, Google Doc, or notes app. We start by asking ourselves, "What do I desire?"

As I sat with that question, staring at an open page in my notebook, I was surprised at how quickly things started coming up.

I wanted the truth.
I wanted justice.
I wanted specific people to repent.
I wanted reconciliation.
I wanted to heal.

I had to learn to hold space for the tension between saying what I want and realizing it isn't the same as getting what I want. In some ways, hope is the space between those two competing narratives. Hope is the liminal vulnerability that invites us into a place where we show up as our whole selves and admit we are limited. We can't undo the past. We can't make people change their minds. We don't get a do-over. The beauty of hope is that we come to it even as we know this and acknowledge no guarantees. We hope for better. We hope for good. We hope, and that is everything.

When we live with the full assurance of hope, we start to desire more goodness for ourselves and others. Our tolerance expands, and our need to control shrinks. We learn to trust ourselves as we discover that our vulnerability strengthens us. As research professor and author Brené Brown noted,

"Vulnerability is not winning or losing; it's having the courage to show up and be seen when we have no control over the outcome. Vulnerability is not weakness; it's our greatest measure of courage."[1]

It's the measure of our courage to hope for the kind of goodness that would feel like the peace of heaven coming to earth, touching our pain, and turning it into something beautiful. A moment requiring our courage is often when uncertainty takes the wheel and drives hope off a cliff. Our instinct to survive amps up and our inner protector parts start hearing warning sirens and attempt to keep us safe by shutting down our desire for hope. If we want to experience the fullness of hope within our grief process, we must acknowledge the risks involved and choose to move forward safely and lovingly. We don't need to rush ourselves here. If we do, we risk missing key healing steps along the way. No benefit comes from running through the process as if it were a race. Hope requires that we live embodied; to do that, we must ensure we are aligned with our body, mind, and spirit. Stay the course. Trust the process.

As my friend Joby Martin said, "If the tomb is empty, then anything is possible."[2]

If the core tenet of Christianity holds that Jesus rose from the grave, leaving his tomb empty, then who are we to decide what is and isn't possible for God?

If the tomb is empty, isn't truth possible? Isn't justice possible? Isn't healing possible? Isn't reconciliation possible?

The answer simply must be yes.

The empty tomb means he is risen. The empty tomb means death is not the end of the story. The empty tomb means our hope has merit, what we want is valid, and goodness in the future is possible because the resurrection brings certainty.

I love what pastor Andy Stanley says about this: "If someone predicts their own death and resurrection and pulls it off, I go with whatever that person says."[3]

History tells us that Jesus wasn't the first to claim he was the Messiah. In fact, many religious and political leaders have visited the ancient Near East and made similar claims. However, their religious movements stopped when the government or unbelievers killed them for their heresy.

Until Jesus.

When he died, the government expected the Jesus movement to die with him. But then he changed everything and conquered death. As author Barbara Johnson wrote, his resurrection encouraged his disciples to live as "Easter people living in a Good Friday world."[4] Because Jesus conquered death, we can live as people of hope and resurrection in a world where good and innocent people get hurt.

This makes me think of something I experienced several years ago. Not long after I joined the staff at Willow, I was walking out of the church one Sunday when a community member called to me from the parking lot. He reached into his pockets, grabbed a set of keys, and threw them my way. When I caught them, I noticed the words *Ferrari Spider*, so I did the most responsible thing and reached into my pocket to throw him the keys to my 2004 Honda Civic. Ha!

He told me to take the Ferrari for the weekend. I was like, "No way am I driving this!" He was persistent and said, "Just take it for a few hours and give your son a ride." So I got in and tried not to freak out as he showed me how to operate it. Before taking it on the road, I did a few practice circles in the empty parking lot. As I was driving, he called me on my cell. I didn't pick up because I was driving a car worth more than everything I owned. He called again, and I anxiously put him on speaker.

"You're driving a V12, supercharged, 788-horsepower Ferrari Spider that goes zero to sixty in less than three seconds—hit the gas!"

I laughed and gave it a few seconds of speed before taking it back down a notch. Still, it was an exceptionally excellent thrill. I missed the rush when I traded it back to him and retrieved my Civic with its kids' sippy cups and cereal-encrusted back seats. I wasn't ungrateful for what I had, but I noticed the differences in the experience.

That night, I realized something. The resurrection changes everything, and Paul said the same power that raised Jesus from the grave is within each of us (Romans 8:11). It's as if we each have this V12 supercharged resurrection power flowing through our veins, but we're driving our lives like a V2, hamster-powered, Cheerios-infested Civic.

I don't just desire something good.

I don't just believe anything is possible.

Resurrection brings the certainty to expect that good is on its way.

Romans 8:28 says, "All things work together for good to them that love God" (KJV).

All things. Even when we're grieving, and it feels impossible.

But slowly, I began to hold space for grief *and* hope.

Hope is the confident expectation that good is on its way.

Paul wrote in Romans 5:2–5, "We boast in the hope of the glory of God. Not only so, but we also glory in our sufferings, because we know that suffering produces perseverance; perseverance, character; and character, hope. And hope does not put us to shame."

Remember what ancient Rome taught:

Hardship is coming.
Suffering will happen.
Prepare for it.

There is a lot of wisdom in that way of thinking, but from that point on it becomes problematic:

Don't trust anyone but yourself.
Hope is weak. It's meaningless.
Reason and reality are your God.

When Paul said that we must persevere and prioritize character development, the church in Rome would have nodded in agreement. However, when he said that everything produces a hope that no one can shame, he lost them. A statement like that was groundbreaking. He was reframing, reminding, and reclaiming the sheer goodness of hope. He was daring to hope, and we can too.

D–Desire something good.
A–Anything is possible.
R–Resurrection brings certainty.
E–Expect good is on its way.

Friend, as we dive deeper into our grief stories, I want us to make room for the possibility of hope as we strive for vulnerability. I know this can be scary and difficult at first, but it's helpful to remember that it is OK to want to hope, heal, be happy again, love again, and try again. I so badly want for you to be able to experience the good in your life again. We can *desire* something good, decide that *anything* is possible, trust that the *resurrection* brings certainty, and *expect* that good is coming.

Reflection Questions

1. What prevents you from the possibility of hope today?
2. Is there one way you can try to DARE to hope this week? Be specific and intentional about creating this goal and commit to it.
3. What comes to mind for you when you think about the concept of vulnerability? What has changed and why?

CHAPTER 5

SPADURA

What Is a SPADURA?

The best definition of *leadership* I've ever read was by Napoleon, who said, "The role of any leader is to define reality and give hope."[1]

We define reality by acknowledging what is true in the here and now. We may be tempted to project our desired reality, but it's important to make sure we are being honest with ourselves about what is our present reality.

After I experienced the fallout at Willow, people often asked me why and how I could still love the church despite what happened to me there. I would quickly stop them and say,

"Willow didn't hurt me. Five people did." Every problem is a people problem. Sometimes we make generalizations or create false narratives that stunt the grieving process. But when you define reality and put a name to the source of your wound, a sacred movement toward healing is unlocked within.

Early on, I struggled with this. I felt that if I named the people who had caused harm, I was either making others see them in a negative light or, equally as hard, admitting that they hurt me. It was easier to paint with broader strokes. By not defining the hurt, abuse, and pain, I couldn't be entirely free and healed from the effects of their decisions. I've struggled to define my reality. It was hard to name my emotions. I honestly felt I couldn't control where these feelings took me. So I worked very hard to keep them bottled up, managed, and put away on the top shelf, believing it would make these feelings taste better someday.

I reached out to a former mentor with some grief counseling background. He'd been one of the first to contact with me when everything went down. When we spoke, he could sense an emotional block within me, and asked, "How's honoring the SPADURA going?"

"Huh?" I said.

I thought he had learned some new Greek or Hebrew words and was testing me. "What kind of gibberish are you talking about?"

That's when he introduced me to the legendary work of the Swiss-American psychiatrist Elisabeth Kübler-Ross. In 1969, she unveiled the five stages of grief (denial, anger, bargaining, depression, acceptance) in her book *On Death and Dying*, based on her work helping those who were terminally ill.[2] This became widely accepted as the standard protocol for the grief process. Over time, what was based on her work with the terminally ill started to resonate with other types of suffering. As it was adapted, two more stages of grief were added, creating what my mentor referred to as the relentless defining of the spiraling realities of SPADURA:

Shock. Also known as *denial*, this is when we struggle to accept the change we've encountered after a disruption. We find it nearly impossible to make sense of all our feelings, thoughts, and emotions and attempt to avoid reality. We say to ourselves, *When will I wake up from this bad dream?*

Pain. As the shock wears off, we begin to feel the pain we've been avoiding. We ask ourselves questions like, *Could I have done more? Should I have spent more time, tried harder, spoken up sooner?* and so on. These questions are natural and essential to the healing process as we work through our pain and grief, staying present and avoiding unhealthy escapes.

Anger. When we begin to feel the pain in the aftermath of our loss, it is common to experience intense anger. Often, we feel resentment for having to go through the grief of what happened to us. We sometimes beg and plead for a second chance to reverse the outcome of our loss or make promises to change if only we could bring our life back to how it once was.

Depression. During this time we finally realize the magnitude of our loss and can feel empty and full of despair. We begin to feel the heaviness of our emotions. *She left. He's gone.*

GRIEVE BREATHE RECEIVE

The job is over. The relationship is different. The disease is fatal. This part of the process can feel terrifying, but it is necessary and won't last forever. Without feeling the depth of our loss, we cannot truly heal from our grief.

Upward Turn. As we start to adjust to our new reality after loss, we enter a middle ground in the healing process. Our ache is still heavy, but our depression starts to lift slightly, and we begin to sense a change of season might be coming.

Reconstruction. We begin making practical decisions for our life after loss, taking active steps to initiate what is required for our new reality. We often feel inspired and determined during this time of rebuilding.

Acceptance. This is the ultimate both/and stage for our grief. We can talk about the weightiness of our loss and have hope for the good that is to come in our future.

So how's honoring the SPADURA going?

We'd talk often, my mentor and I, and as he'd check in about my SPADURA process, I'd take inventory of where in the stages I found myself. It took me awhile to realize this wasn't going to be a literal progression of stages. At first, I looked at it as a map to take me from A to B. Do everything right, check each box, get to the end, and—*yay, I'm healed!* But grief doesn't work like that. At any moment, we can encounter something triggering. Sometimes the trigger can be a memory or something someone says that hits different, or we might read something online that sends us spinning.

For me, working through the SPADURA felt like living in a life-size emotional pinball machine. At one moment,

54

I'd feel shock or denial because I couldn't believe this was happening to me, and then in an instant, I'd feel profound sadness that kept me from leaving my bed. My loneliness often brought up feelings of anger. Sometimes I'd attempt to bargain with God, grasping for anything that might give me back what I'd lost.

Defining my emotional reality became my work to do. Learning to slow myself down so I could actively identify where in the SPADURA I was became essential. I knew choosing unhealthy escapes and staying stuck in my fear would prolong my suffering. If I refused to move through the process of honoring what I'd lived through, I wouldn't be able to access the peace and hope I so desperately desired.

My counselor would often say, "Slow is smooth, and smooth is fast," a reference to a phrase used by firefighters. If they wind the firehoses too quickly, they form kinks that can damage the integrity of the hoses, preventing them from doing their job when needed. The stages of grief require us to slow down so that we can identify where we are in the healing process. Attempts to skip or bypass parts of this time by rushing can cause kinks—more delays and struggle in our recovery down the road.

One of the verses I returned to often says, "Above all else, guard your heart, for everything you do flows from it" (Proverbs 4:23). If slow is smooth, and smooth is fast, then it's vital to take our time so that what flows out from our hearts at the end of the SPADURA is whole, healthy, and full of hope.

Using the word *guard* in Proverbs 4:23 is an interesting

choice. We guard our personal information, taking care not to expose our email or social media login and keeping our Social Security number private. We guard our time, keeping calendars and blocking space for the things we want to do most. We guard our valuables, arming cars with alarm systems and installing security cameras at our homes. We tend to protect the things we value, but how often do we guard our hearts? The Hebrew word translated as "guard" is *natsar*, which means to relentlessly defend and guard what matters most from danger.[3] Picture the defensive wizardry of NBA basketball star Patrick Beverley—that's the kind of fierce energy this verse wants us to bring to the table when it comes to guarding our hearts.

In my quest for a better understanding of grief as well as healing, I spent time learning more about what it takes to guard our hearts. During that time, I developed a simple practice we can move through by activating the following four prompts:

Play It Honest (Respect). I commit to defining my emotional reality and playing the upcoming week emotionally honest. I choose not to hide, stuff, push away, minimize, or use anything as an excuse to run toward an unhealthy escape. I commit to honoring what's going on in my heart. Our feelings have a motion to them, which is why they're called emotions.

Play It Back (Reflect). I look at the last week and identify one or two times when I didn't guard my heart or chose not to define my emotional reality. I try not to focus on what I did but instead on what was happening underneath the surface.

Why am I feeling anxious, stressed, tired, frustrated, disappointed, or some other emotion that caused me not to want to do the work of defining my emotional reality? I write about what caused that feeling.

Play It Out (Rewrite). I look ahead to the upcoming week and imagine myself back in that same situation, but this time, instead of reenacting the past, I rewrite what a Christ-centered response could be. I try it on. I visualize it. I practice my answer. I say it out loud. I define my emotional reality as doing it in real time with my wife or close friends.

Play It Smart (Refuel). If everything flows from my heart, I must intentionally refuel my heart with time. The more moments I refuel, the easier I find it is to access the parts of me that have been buried for a long time. Schedule the hike. Call the friend. Go out for coffee. Listen to the podcast. Look for healthy escapes that will bring joy to your soul.

Grieving the gap between what had become my reality and what I thought my life would look like was impossibly hard. It stretched me to my limit as I tried to honor the memories and feelings they stirred, essentially embracing what came up when change appeared in my life. We often don't know what to do with such high emotional and spiritual pain. We default to management tactics to keep it palatable and minimize our wounds to help them feel survivable.

Our bodies betray all our best efforts, though, because our bodies know better than to let us try to skip over the healing we need. This plays out in many ways as our bodies absorb our trauma, including symptoms such as backaches, muscle spasms, migraines, and panic attacks. Often we are more likely to get sick when we're in a survival state, even the smallest of bugs laying us out for days longer as we recover. It's our body's way of screaming, "Listen to me! You can't keep pretending nothing bad has happened here."

If we are committed to healing, then we must also be committed to our health, mentally and physically. Does this mean we all need to get gym memberships and start eating kale? Of course not. I wouldn't wish kale on anyone, not even my worst enemies. What it does mean, though, is we've got to take care of ourselves. We must intentionally nurture our whole selves, bodies included. Depending on your mobility and capacity, this may look like taking a daily walk or choosing to cook fresh food at home a few more days each week. Having a standing lunch or phone date with a loved one is another form of caring for ourselves. Perhaps we treat ourselves to a new book or make a new playlist. As long as it brings us joy and fills us up, all of this counts as care!

Honoring the SPADURA is how we honor ourselves. It's a way to make sure we don't leave ourselves behind, stuck in a pit of grief and loss. Choosing to embrace the process and submit to the slow and smooth way of grief allows us to reach out and grasp the hope we each so desperately long for. If you find yourself in the midst of this GBR Journey, I want you to know that you are not alone, and you will get through it. You will find peace and hope and a whole new chapter of your life as you focus on caring for and nurturing your heart.

Reflection Questions

1. Where in the SPADURA do you find yourself right now?
2. What is one way you can treat yourself this week? Write it down and be sure to follow through on it. Your future self will thank you!
3. What can you do to better guard your heart in this season?

CHAPTER 6

PUNCHING PILLOWS

What Are You So Mad About?

For several years, my friend Brad has been hosting groups of people in leadership roles at a dude ranch deep in the mountains of Colorado. I had the chance to attend the year after I resigned from Willow. I was nervous as I walked into a packed room with leaders and pastors whose names I knew and deeply respected. As unsure as I was that I belonged in the same room with such incredible people, I also recognized a similarity we all shared—in each of our stories, we were supposed to be stepping into roles with more responsibility, such as succession. However, the wheels had flown off for us for many reasons. I was sure Brad had planned this particular group intentionally, and something about that idea gave me hope and helped me feel more comfortable as I found my seat beside them.

Each year, Brad invites a few "old dogs" to attend and share their advice on how leaders might finish the race well, step into their responsibilities with wisdom, and lead from a place of strength and clarity. For this session, a pastor named Darrin Patrick came to share his life, struggles, and career rise and fall with us. He also shared vulnerably about what he viewed as the redemption story God was writing in his life. His courage and humility to publicly own his failings stood in stark contrast to what I'd witnessed during my time at Willow.

Darrin took vulnerability to another level and outlined ways he was actively working on making amends with those he had deeply wounded due to how he lived. He had sat with his former staff as they shared ways he had hurt them and their community and chose to simply listen and not defend as person after person expressed their pain and anger. Darrin knew that if he wanted a chance to heal these relationships, he needed to embrace the reality of the collateral damage done to them and their families.

I was on the edge of my seat as he shared, genuinely surprised by his honesty and the extent to which he let us into his story. A sense of desire was stirring as I wondered what it would feel like to hear similar words of ownership and repentance from the people who had hurt me. I broke down in tears as I listened to his account, unsure I would ever get the chance. There was a weight in the room as I looked from face to face. I was not the only one touched by this moment. Perhaps I was also not the only one reflecting on past wounds, wishing for opportunities for confrontation, accountability, and reconciliation with those who'd harmed us.

Darrin also noticed the energy change and contacted a few of us after the session ended. He invited us to keep the conversation going at his cabin, and while I knew it would be a beneficial time, I was also afraid. I wasn't sure I could be honest with Darrin, the other leaders, or myself. I had gotten so good at keeping the secrets, pain, and details I knew about how others had misbehaved at Willow, yet these things were eating me up from the inside. I knew what was at stake if some information fell into the wrong hands. But as I looked at the faces around me, I realized that each of us was holding similar secrets. The wounds in my heart looked a lot like the wounds in theirs. We each had been programmed to protect the institution of the church at all costs, even and especially at the expense of our well-being.

Could we speak that truth out loud, be trusted, and handle the ugly, the anger, and the pain? So much of my spirit was afraid to let others in. Maybe they would think I was wrong. Maybe they would shun, shame, or even hate me. Perhaps they wouldn't believe me, questioning my memories and motivation. Those kinds of things had happened to me during the past year, so my fear wasn't out of the realm of possibility. I wasn't sure I could bear that sort of rejection from people I respected so highly. We all tentatively agreed to at least try as we began the trek to Darrin's bungalow.

That evening in the mountains became a catalyst for profound healing. Darrin allowed us to engage in honest conversations, each of us sharing as we felt led. Stories of our anger and shame and sorrow, grief upon grief. One at a time, we listened, honored, and encouraged one another as we let the weight we'd been carrying fall off our shoulders.

We continued the conversation over the next few weeks with texts and phone calls. A sort of trauma bond had been formed between us, and the integrity of these new friendships was further enforced with each new story shared. I had no idea how much that time would come to mean to me as the following weeks unfolded.

One morning, a new text popped up in our shared thread: "I can't believe this, but I've just been told that Darrin died."

It was so sudden. We'd been texting with him just days before this news. What could have happened to our friend? Had he been sick? Was he in a car accident? The details weren't precise, but the math wasn't adding up. In the coming days, we learned that Darrin had died by suicide. The shock of this was palpable. None of us had seen it coming. We knew he had faced some demons but had no clue things had ever been that dark.

Months later, two of the friends from that group reached out. They had an idea they couldn't shake. They wanted to create a cohort designed to cultivate an experience similar to what we'd had in that cabin in the mountains of Colorado.

After realizing the benefit of this work of facing our trauma and healing, they longed to walk alongside other leaders who were drifting toward isolation. They wanted to create spaces for others to find community, heal, embrace vulnerability, and get the care needed to prevent such a horrible and sad outcome. If Darrin had been struggling so badly and we didn't know, how many other people were in similar situations? And what if we could do something—make something—that could help them?

Out of those questions came the 10Ten Project, a yearlong journey of adventure, exploration of the soul, and radical transparency.[1] I had the honor of being a member of their cohort, and it was one of the most meaningful and personal experiences for me during that time of my life. As part of the 10Ten Project cohort, we went for one week to a counseling intensive called Onsite.[2] We were asked to stay off our cell phones and abstain from alcohol and other unhealthy escapes that would prevent us from being present during our time there. I didn't know what to expect and felt a little nervous about how deep and genuine they'd expect us to get with one another in just a week.

Twelve of us were linked together in this cohort experience. In the beginning, we were told our time in the group sessions would be unlike anything we had ever done (a fact that ended up being the understatement of the year!). The counselor we were connected with was a gentleman named Jim. This guy must have been a Jedi because his ability to disarm even the most formidable characters was otherworldly.

He was also creative, using props to illustrate his points and always knowing the perfect questions to ask to draw us out of our comfort zones and into our vulnerability.

A few of us would sit in the hot seat with Jim in every session while the rest of the group looked on. As we would share our experiences, Jim would get a sense of what was needed to uncover the pain we weren't yet able to tap into, to be able to grieve it and lay it down. It was as if Jim was listening to where the Spirit was taking the conversation, and then once he got a sense of the direction, he would take it to the next level. He would utilize his prop box and guide the person speaking to enter a sort of reenactment of the scene of their trauma. Sometimes it was to immerse ourselves in the moment or memory so we could feel it, and sometimes he asked us to reimagine the scene as if what we had wished had happened. Other group members would often be invited to role-play characters in the scene. It felt odd at first, but we realized how powerful and moving it could be to revisit old memories to bring perspective and healing.

Toward the end of the week, my name was called to sit in the hot seat with Jim. I had seen enough moments as my fellow participants had gone before me to know this would be a challenging and enriching experience, but my nerves were instantly on guard. Jim asked me a handful of questions about what had led me to that moment, where I sensed my pain was coming from, and what I wanted to do about it. As I spoke, I knew my heart was guarded, and I wasn't letting Jim see the real me. I was scared of what it would feel like to give up control and trust someone else, even just for this simple exercise. Of course, Jim the Jedi picked up on this; before long, he had zeroed in on it. He could tell that I wasn't in touch with my sadness and anger and that I was holding back. I'll never forget when he graciously asked me, "Steve, do you think we need to have a conversation with Bill?"

"With?" I eked out, barely above a whisper. *Oh God, no.* This wasn't going to be one of those talk-show moments where they bring the person out from backstage, was it? I felt frozen in an instant panic. Thankfully, that wasn't the plan. It's wild, though, how our minds leap to fight-or-flight the instant we feel threatened. Jim explained that we would have someone from the group role-play Bill so I could look him in the eye and play out what I would want to say if Bill were there. I took a deep breath. I knew I wanted to say some things to Bill, but I was afraid of what those words would be.

As I turned to face my friend, who was now pretending to be Bill, I felt the adrenaline rush up my spine. I tried to say what I wanted to and get the words out:

"How could you?"

"You have ruined my life!"

"You are disgusting!"

"How could you ever harm those women, their families, and wreck their lives forever because you couldn't control yourself?!"

"You are the biggest narcissistic, selfish, ego-driven jerk and have no right to call yourself a pastor!"

My words, while loaded, still fell flat. Even as I spoke the words, I knew I couldn't access the fullness of my rage and grief. Jim knew it too. He knew there was more, much more. I needed to get out. We wrapped up the scene, the guy role-playing Bill returned to being my friend, and I hoped there were no hard feelings. (Of course there weren't, but that's just how uncomfortable I was with my anger. Even pretend fights felt like too much. I had a lot of work to do.)

Next, Jim directed our group members to scour the building and collect every cushion and pillow. We all started stacking the cushions and pillows into an altar-like fort.

After a few minutes of stacking, he took a step back to admire our work and proudly exclaimed, "Yeah, that's about right!" He looked at me and said, "I need you to know it's OK to get in touch with your anger. You're safe here." Then he looked at each person and said, "Am I right? Steve is fully safe to access his anger, right?"

Every head nodded.

Then Jim said to me, "I'm going to ask you a question, and when you answer, I give you full permission to hit these cushions as hard as humanly possible. Deal?"

I responded with, "I think so."

Then Jedi Jim said, "So what did Bill take from you?"

I looked at him, bewildered. Before I could answer, he gently pointed to the cushion altar. Then he stood behind me and placed his hands on my shoulders. "Steve, he took a lot from you. You don't need to carry this anymore. You're safe here. Let it rip!"

I took a deep breath, keeping his question front and center

in my mind. What did Bill take from me? My kids' faces flashed in my mind, and then Sarah's, their tears and sadness as we moved away from the home they'd known and loved. I let my fists fly. I could feel tears streaming down my face as things came up.

My career.
My congregation.
My integrity.
My confidence.
My home.
My friends.
My dreams.
My trust.
My energy.
My ambition.
My security.
My plans.
My influence.
My future.

Everything stood still for several minutes as I punched, screamed, kicked, and ugly-cried through every question. Sweating and heaving, I slowly stopped and let myself stand very still. My mind was numb, and my heart was racing, but I felt calm. A peace washed over me that I hadn't felt since I learned of the accusations against Bill. I had been so exhausted, angry, scared, and disillusioned for so long. All of that had been in me, brewing and stirring with no way out. How had I not known it until now?

As the room remained silent, I became aware of how out of control I had become, and a flash of embarrassment rose. *I shouldn't have done that, let my guard down, and let them see me like that.* But before the shame storm could take over, Jim and the group surrounded me. I can't even imagine what they were thinking after what they had just witnessed, but they embraced me at that moment, just as I was: a grieving, angry mess. Then they each looked me in the eye and spoke a word over me, words of faith and love that made the shame run for the hills.

The SPADURA is not linear but more spiral, with certain moments demanding we honor the ache and give up the pretense that we are invincible. On that day in the cohort, anger needed my attention. It needed some room to exist without shame, management, or judgment. That exercise ushered forth a deep engagement into the caverns of my anger. I realized I was still carrying a lot of rage inside, and I knew the next phase of this healing process would help me prepare to let it all go.

Good grief happens when we allow ourselves to feel the entire expanse of our needs. Good grief occurs when we stop shaming the parts we wish weren't true and instead make room for them. Good grief is the chance to reunite with our pain, seeing it as our friend and teacher rather than an exile.

Reflection Questions

1. As you read this chapter, what came to mind when you processed your own personal understanding of anger? How did it change?
2. Has there been a time in your life when you've experienced grief as good? What was that like and how can you learn from it now?
3. Do you have an old memory that could benefit by revisiting it, sitting with it, and bringing an opportunity for healing to it?

PART 2

BREATHE

Welcome to *Saturday*.

We now know the value of understanding and honoring the ways that grief and change travel together through our life. Oftentimes, they appear like a twisted and knotted thread, emotion and shock tangled together, making it nearly impossible to figure out where one ends and the other begins. There is nothing more essential to a human being than air. With every second, we are sustaining our life. Inhale. Exhale. In. Out. Over and over and over again. Like change, breath is an essential foundation of life. As we breathe in, our body undergoes a physical transformation. We filter oxygen through our lungs, pushing it into our blood as it nourishes our cells. At the same time, our every exhale is pushing carbon dioxide out, expelling toxins from our body. With every breath, the air has changed us, fueled us, and left us better.

Breathe asks us to pause. To slow it all down. To sit in our pain and not avoid it. To traverse this part of the trail well, we will need to make safe spaces within our lives to do the work it requires. Personally, I found my space in the desert. It was a place where I could strip away the extra layers of baggage I'd been carrying for way too long. For you, it might look like choosing to journal on the train ride to work rather than dive into the latest podcast. The gift of *Breathe* is that as you travel, each breath goes in and out, right through you. Focusing on our breathing helps us through our grief; it slows the inner noise and helps us learn how to honor the waiting.

We've trod some hard ground in the territory of *Grieve*, and now it's time to create the space to step into another part of our GBR Journey, the valleys of *Breathe*.

THE GRIEF JOURNEY

GRIEVE
The Journey
In Grief

CHANGE

BREATHE
The Journey
Through Grief

CHAPTER 7

STACKING STONES

What Do I Do Now?

There is nothing like the desert.

It gets its name from being the deserted place or, better said, a place for the deserted.

For centuries people have made their way to the deserted place in search of something. I wonder if this is why the best rehab facilities all seem to be in the desert. But let's be honest. Nobody ever wants to go to the desert. It tends to be a last resort for when you feel forsaken, alone, and at the end of your rope.

Years ago, I met a rabbi in Jerusalem, and we got to

talking about the three significant landmarks in the Hebrew scriptures: Egypt, the desert, and the promised land. At one point, I asked him how long people usually stay in each of these places.

He looked at me and said, "You Americans are so funny. You assume somebody will live most of their life in the promised land, but we are different. We believe that people will spend ten to fifteen percent of their life in Egypt, ten to fifteen percent in the promised land, and the remaining seventy to eighty percent in the desert." When he said this, I can't even imagine what my face must have looked like. I didn't fully comprehend the weight of what he was sharing. It wasn't until much later, after I moved to the desert myself, that I began to gain a profound understanding of the wisdom this rabbi had shared with me.

After I had resigned in protest from Willow, people were angry. People were sad. People wanted answers. The church leaders had not told the whole story, preferring to keep themselves managed by lawyers and PR firms and safe from lawsuits and liability. They used the same playbook that has been used to keep corrupt leaders safe from accountability and effectively left the congregation to puzzle out the truth alone and without all the pieces.

Shortly after stepping away, I took Emerson, who was ten at the time, with me on a coffee run to our local spot. As we entered the shop, I immediately felt looks and glares from people who knew who I was. The air was thick with emotion. I put my arm around Emerson, shielding him from the unspoken anger. We ordered our usual drinks, and as we made our way to the end of the counter to wait for our order, a woman came up and started screaming at me.

"You're a coward! You abandoned us. You're not a leader. You should be ashamed of yourself. You're a disgrace!"

I stood very still, weighing my options. I'll never forget my son taking my hand, looking at me, looking at this woman. She did not want an explanation. She wasn't interested in hearing my side of things. She was livid and had already filled in the details of what she assumed about what happened at Willow, and I was just her verbal punching bag. The barista called my name, and I quickly grabbed our drinks and headed out the door.

I turned to Emerson and brought him in for a hug. I was surprised to realize both of us were shaking. I said, "Oh, pal. I am sorry you had to hear that."

He looked back at me and said, "Dad, you always told me it's important to do the right thing in life. You even said we get rewarded for doing the right thing. But that lady was mad, which makes me wonder, did you do the right thing? Or did you lie when you said you will always be rewarded for doing the right thing?"

My heart broke as I considered his question. I know we don't always get what we want, and there have been plenty of times when we do what's right and don't experience any praise or reward for it.

As we drove home, I looked at him and said, "When your mom was pregnant with your little sister, she threw up multiple times a day. It was a tough pregnancy. Some days, she couldn't get out of bed. It was brutal. But when we met Mercy for the first time, it was all worth it. I can't tell you it's going to be easy, and I can't give you a timeline, but I do believe there will be a moment someday when we will hold our version of mercy in this situation because we did the right thing and spoke up for the people who were hurt."

Still, most nights, I struggled with sleep. Anxiety would bubble up and flood my mind with worry and fear. One night, I woke up at about 3:00 a.m. with my heart racing. I was sweating and breathing heavily as if I'd just run miles. I guess I *was* running from something. I didn't want to face the question rising from deep within: *What do we do now?* I had a sneaking suspicion that we couldn't stay where we were, my having made the gut-wrenching decision to resign without a plan B rather than compromise my support of the victims.

As a result, my world fell apart, and my dreams came crashing down like a house of cards. I felt a visceral yearning to do something. I wanted to distract myself from what felt like an impossible grief. I had an intuitive push to throw myself into achievement. I wanted to keep myself busy by finding something new and impressive to do. Where could I go to escape the sadness, to distract myself from feeling the weightiness of the betrayal and trauma? A bigger city? A bigger role? I was looking for anything that would make it all feel worth what I had to endure.

Yet deep within, I knew what I was doing. I was still trying to escape from my pain.

As I lay in bed watching the sun crack through the backyard fence, I knew I couldn't achieve my way out of this. I knew better than to think a quick fix would repair what had been broken in me.

I got out of bed and went to the living room. Looking out the window, I sensed an internal whisper: *Go to the desert and wait for instructions.*

It was so calm and firm and "other" that I grabbed my journal and wrote down that phrase. I sat in silence and considered this prompting about the desert. I was not a desert kind of guy. I grew up in California and spent my free time surfing the coast. The desert appealed to me about as much as staying put did at that moment. This was a metaphorical desert, right? A still, small voice I recognized as God's rumbled within: *You can't achieve your way out of this. You can only grieve your way through it.*

One by one, all the plans I'd been trying to arrange, all the efforts I'd begun to make to strategize for what was next, all the cities I'd been googling and searching aimlessly on Zillow—all of it started to evaporate. I didn't know much beyond the clear sense that God was calling us to some kind of desert. What we needed was less, not more. Less spotlight, less fame, less pressure, less performance. We needed a place that was safe and off the radar. I knew then that I would not be taking on another leadership role. I wouldn't accept any offer to move to another church and be the senior pastor. I was broken because of what I'd experienced and needed recovery before thinking about leading again.

Later, as the house began to stir and my family began to wake, I brewed a pot of coffee and filled two mugs, bringing one to my wife, sitting on the patio. As steam rose from her cup, I tried to think of how to tell her what I'd heard the night before. How would she react? I knew she'd grown attached to our home and neighborhood. I knew there was a big chance she would look at me like I'd lost my mind to even think of not taking another job, any job, that would keep the paychecks coming. I took a breath and took a chance, telling her the words I'd heard whispered to me from within. Before I even finished the sentence, she teared up. I was worried she was upset, but she smiled.

She looked at me and whispered, "I've been sensing the same thing. I want to go home."

It hit me at that moment: God wasn't telling us to go to some metaphorical place. We would move to the literal desert, to my wife's home state of Arizona. The fact that we'd both been sensing the same thing confirmed it was the next right step for our family.

After we moved to Phoenix, I began to travel to various churches and events guest speaking at weekend services and conferences. In my spare time, I decided to really get into hiking. I'd wake up every morning and find a new trail to discover. I loved Eugene Peterson's words, "All theology is rooted in geography,"[1] and used them as a framework for the new location we called home. I'd heard of a community of third-century Egyptian monks known as the Desert Fathers and Mothers who left the bustle of the city and retreated to the forsaken and deserted place. I wanted to learn all I could from them, so I picked up every book I could find.

I sought out the dusty trails, brown terrain, dry heat, and wide-open spaces free of cement. I experienced temperatures hotter than temperatures should ever be. I had to adjust to shaking out my shoes before putting them on because scorpions were real. I had to adjust to the howls of coyotes outside my window every night. The desert was different from any environment I'd ever lived in, and I knew it would be the right backdrop as I started the work of facing the forsaken places within me.

My whole life had been a quest to bypass the desert—the lonely, the boring, the mundane. I've never been afraid of hard work, but I was scared of feeling pain, anger, and any other socially unacceptable emotions. So I avoided them. I arranged my life by calculating risks, staying in control, working harder, wanting to get better, and always knowing where I was going next, believing it would lead me to the promised land. My life had been, up until that point, highly focused and goal-oriented, like a good stock market graph where the trajectory kept moving up and to the right. I had been living as if my achievements were squarely centered in God's will.

While hiking on a trail, my son's words would often rise in my head: "You said you will always be rewarded for doing the right thing . . ." Did I still believe that was true? Had my paradigm for life been off its axis, tilted slightly and spinning in God's orbit, but not completely? I still had a long way to go, but I was starting to see that the ways I'd been living required an adjustment, whether I'd ever left Willow or moved to Arizona. Whether I'd admit it or not. I had to let myself lose control and tap into the emotions I'd spent so much energy pushing away.

One early morning, as I stood at the top of the Apache Wash Loop Trail, it all hit me. With the sun rising in the distance, I broke down. I let myself start to grieve the reality of what was true. I had to admit that what had happened had hurt me. They had hurt me. I wasn't invincible. I couldn't keep running, hiding, pretending I was fine, and hoping to convince myself it was true. The truth was, I was deeply wounded spiritually and emotionally, and the people who had done it seemed unaffected.

Just the thought of that shook me and left me breathing shallowly. I took a few grounding steps and bent down on the trail. I didn't want vengeance and wasn't looking for someone to blame. I wanted to figure out a way to heal. I realized that in much of my life I hadn't done the work of healing. Perhaps I'd merely slapped a Band-Aid on my gushing wounds and called it good. I had moved on, achieved more, filled my calendar, and assumed my wounds would mend on their own over time. What would happen if I tried to relinquish control and allow God to heal me wholly? I felt the only way to find out was to consent to reality and finally choose to surrender by submitting to the process.

I grabbed a handful of rocks and began prayerfully stacking them, one on top of the other, until they formed a little tower. As I built that small altar on the side of the trail, I thought of a friend of mine. He had also gone through a dark and complex period that left him in a similar place, aching and unsure of what to do next. I remember him saying that for months he would walk his property every day searching for large stones to use for a perimeter wall. The first two months, he was so angry that for every rock he picked up, he pictured someone who had wronged him and cursed them as he settled the stone into the ground. In months three and four, his angst turned to God as he wondered, *How did you let this happen to me?* And finally, as the wall grew in the last few months, he waved the white flag of surrender and simply prayed, *What is it within me that needs to heal, Lord? I give up trying to run from it.*

While my pain is personal, the ache is universal. Have you ever found yourself asking similar questions? We are not alone in our struggle with control or our fear of the cost of healing. Personally, I didn't want to stay stuck and unwell. I wanted to heal and move through the process God was inviting me into. I wanted to wake up someday on the other side of my grief.

There was something about making a tangible object that signaled to my brain that this was real. What I was feeling was real. What I had lived through was real. What I had to grieve the loss of was real too. The same is true for you, dear reader. What you were feeling was real. What you lived through was real. What you had to grieve the loss of was real too. And if the loss and the grief were real, that means the healing and hope might be too. That was a promise I'd cling to in the coming months as I started my healing journey with God, letting him mend years of untreated emotional wounds. I'd attempted to bypass the proverbial desert, which meant that the majority of my life I'd been avoiding the very invitation that would help me grow. Now I was learning not to fear the difficulty and desolation of the inner desert, but to welcome and embrace it. The desert was making room for everything my heart, soul, mind, and body needed to access in order to get well.

Reflection Questions

1. What in you needs to heal today? What is one tangible step you can take to begin that process?
2. Have you ever had an experience where you felt called to something? What was that like and how did you know?

CHAPTER 8

BET IT ALL

Is Anything Hazardous in There?

There's an old card game called seven-up that the early settlers used to play. The premise was low card always wins. In the White Mountains of Arizona during the 1870s, the properties belonging to two ranchers started encroaching on each other. The legend says the two ranchers decided to sit at a table and play the game; the winner would take the other's property.

Marion Clark told Corydon E. Cooley, "If you can show the low card, you win."

Cooley nodded and then turned his card over, revealing the deuce of clubs. He said, "Show low it is."[1]

One hundred thousand acres of prime real estate became Cooley's, and when it was time to name the new town, he called it Show Low. The main street in the town is named Deuce of Clubs, and supposedly, if there is ever a runoff between two mayoral candidates, they settle it at the table with a game of seven-up in which the low card wins in honor of how the city came to be.

This quirky little town became a bit of a refuge for my family as we tried to find our footing after the events of 2018.

My wife grew up going to Show Low, Arizona, with her family. They'd visit her grandparents and spend days fishing for trout, hiking through the beauty of ponderosa pine forests, and enjoying the cooler mountain temperatures. She always dreamed of having a place there, and we would sometimes look up homes for sale online and daydream about what life in the mountains might be like.

One day while I was traveling for work, my wife called me. "You have to check out the link I just sent you," she said. "I mean, it has to be a typo, right? There's no way. It's too good to be true!"

I opened the link and scrolled photos of a small A-frame cabin settled on three acres just outside of Show Low. The structure was dated and needed some repair, but it was also a steal of a deal. I couldn't believe we'd found something within our meager budget. I knew we had to go check it out.

The next day, Sarah and my in-laws drove three hours

north to meet with the Realtor. As they pulled up, another couple was just leaving their showing. Sarah called me from the gravel driveway after getting all the details. In true Sarah form, she started with the story of the people who owned the home. It had only ever been owned by the sellers, a married couple who'd spent their careers as schoolteachers. They built the place themselves as a labor of love and intention. They never planned to sell it, but their kids had grown and moved away, and there was no one left to leave it to. After the husband passed away, the wife moved into an assisted living home. Even though the house had been listed only the day before, they already had multiple offers above the asking price.

I nodded. I knew there was no way we could compete.

"But," Sarah continued, "she is adamant that the cabin legacy continue on and only wants to sell it to another family who will use it to create memories with their kids for years to come."

"Oh yeah?" I said, trying to sound casual.

"Yep. So I got permission to write to her about my childhood memories and our family. We should put in our offer, even if it isn't competitive. If it is meant to be, it will be," she added.

I felt the same, so we made an offer then and there.

The next day, the Realtor called to congratulate us on our new cabin. We couldn't believe it! It was exciting, but we also knew we were in for a lot of work, most of which we'd have to do ourselves to save money. The adventure was just beginning.

We spent the first year renovating the house. We'd load

up the kids and our dog and drive up the mountain, sleeping on inflatable mattresses in the living room as we ripped out flooring and walls. To be honest, the place was a hot mess. More than twenty years with zero updates meant some core things needed to be overhauled. I learned how to lay tile and wood flooring, and Sarah became a spackling and hardwire lighting expert. We made many trips to Home Depot that summer. I also frequently ran to the Show Low town dump during the demolition.

The official name is the Lone Pine Transfer Station, but let's be honest, *the Show Low town dump* is way more fun to say.

As I drove to the Show Low town dump, I pulled in onto a massive scale that would weigh my car. A little window would open, and a kind older gentleman who called himself "the weighmaster" would take my driver's license.

He'd inspect the trash and ask, "Anything hazardous in there? Because you can't bring hazardous stuff today."

One time, I asked the weighmaster if there was a day when someone could bring hazardous materials, and he told me, "We don't accept anything hazardous here!"

After my car was weighed and inspected, I'd be handed a laminated card with a number and directions to the hangar, where I'd unload our trash. For some reason, this was actually a fun chore for me. Maybe it was because as I'd load up a truckload of trash and discarded building materials, I'd glimpse some progress. The clutter and junk were slowly being cleared away. We actually *were* renovating a cabin in the woods, and it was becoming pretty fantastic. I also had fun throwing all that junk as far up the trash mountain as possible. It was oddly cathartic.

After I emptied our trash, I'd return to the weighmaster and hand him back the laminated card. He would weigh my vehicle again, logging the difference in weight for the fee.

I always felt lighter driving back to the cabin after that.

One night, while I was prepping for an upcoming talk, I came across an article detailing how archaeologists traced Jesus' final hours. As I read, I was blown away by this line: "Although the exact route to the crucifixion is unknown, there is general agreement that it took place at Golgotha, a garbage dump outside Jerusalem."[2]

What the what? Did Jesus die at a town dump? Did Good Friday take place at the Jerusalem town dump? I couldn't put my finger on it just yet, but somehow there was a lesson for me lingering between the Show Low town dump and this new finding about where Jesus died.

Later, during a therapy session, my therapist asked me about my perspective on forgiveness. As I considered what she was asking me, I was surprised by what came up. She let me share for a bit, and then she stopped me. "I can see you are doing really good work to forgive others, but can you tell me about a time when you have forgiven yourself?"

I sat there speechless for a few moments. A flood of memories filled my brain: moments of regret, times I had failed, and fractured relationships I couldn't fully fix. So many memories flashed through my mind, but one in particular hit me hard.

When I left Willow, I was in the middle of a book contract that required me to write two more books. My publisher then came to me shortly after I'd left Willow and talked about writing a book about that experience. That short meeting turned into my leaving for a week to write in Colorado Springs and a team coming to my house in Illinois to gather my story.

The more I wrote, the more my sadness welled up and shifted into anger. I was angry over everything that had been lost. I was angry that the victims had been gaslighted and shunned. I was upset about my fractured relationships because I had chosen to support the victims. I was heartbroken over losing my dream job, because I didn't just lose my job—I lost my connection with a congregation I adored, a mentor I loved, and a staff team I thought I'd work with for the next twenty-five years. My family and I lost our home, friendships, and security.

I was *angry*.

And at that moment, the idea was floated by my publisher to take those feelings and put them in a book. If I did this, the publisher said it would fulfill my contract. They also offered me more money. When I'd tendered my resignation, I did not have a contingency plan. There was no expectation of a severance; I expected to go from a steady paycheck to nothing. So I entertained the offer. My scarcity mentality wanted security. My anger wanted vindication.

Before I could get my head wrapped around what I was doing, the train was in motion. The publisher produced a cover and a URL for preorders within weeks. My anger shifted into anxiety, and panic overtook me. Without my consent, the PR firm hired to help get the word out did its job and told a journalist about the book. I pleaded with them not to move forward, but they did. The article dropped, and I didn't see it coming.

I was not in my right mind to make calls like that. I was in the middle of massive grief, and now I was out of control of the situation, unable to get a retraction or a chance to speak on my own behalf.

News of the book spread.

People preordered it.

It was in the top ten on Amazon sales.

People thought I was just trying to profit off the scandal.

What I had entertained from a place of pain and scarcity ended up hurting more people. I was tired of people not knowing the full story of what happened behind the scenes at Willow. I was sad for all that was lost, and I wanted to make it better. I wanted the social media attacks on my family to stop, and I thought I could set things right with more information. I wanted people to know the truth. But I was in no place mentally, physically, spiritually, or emotionally to write a book back then.

After consideration, I called the publisher and backed out of the contract. They told me the only way I could get out of it was to buy myself out of the contract. I would have to repay my advance in order to stop production of that book and get out of my business relationship with them. I knew my integrity was on the line, and I had to do anything to prevent that book—which read more like an angry journal entry—from coming into the world. I agreed.

My anger and fear cost me a lot of money.

I emptied our family's savings.

Our safety net was gone, and now we truly had nothing left.

My counselor often talks about intention and impact. Often our intention is good, or we're unaware of what's actually driving us, but the impact is felt by those around us. Other times our intention is grounded in negativity, sadness, unforgiveness, and anger, which makes the impact on others more painful. I've definitely done both. The book was grounded in unhealthy intentions, which led to an impact that cost me financially, emotionally, and relationally. I had never dealt with the full reality of my actions around the book. When my counselor talked about forgiving myself, I knew I needed to start there.

Between working on the cabin and flying to various states for work, I found solace in the pine forest of northern Arizona. I got in the habit of carrying a small wooden cross about the size of a quarter around in my pocket every day. Holding it became a comfort as I paced the trails around Show Low, letting thoughts flow and memories come to the surface. I journaled and processed with Sarah and my friends. I realized the toxic and hazardous energy of shame had been pumping through my body for quite some time. I needed healthy outlets for all that was stirring within.

A few weeks later, I pulled my car full of another load of renovation trash up to Weighmaster Tom's window.

"Anything hazardous?" he asked me, glancing sideways. I shook my head, took the laminated card, and headed to the stacks of trash. After I opened the back of the van, I put the key back in my pocket and instantly felt the small wooden cross I'd kept with me during this season. I pulled it out and held it in my hand. Then I lifted it up so it appeared to be standing at the top of the trash heap.

Golgotha.

The foot of the cross is where all my toxic and hazardous shame, regret, and sins belong. It's the place where I don't have to explain or reason. I can just lay it down and leave it behind.

With each piece of debris I tossed from the back of my car, I thought of places in my story where I'd failed to forgive myself.

And then, I forgave myself.

Golgotha, *for me.*
Good Friday, *for me.*
Holy Saturday, *for me.*
Resurrection Sunday, *for me.*

I'm sure I looked like a madman as I pulled back up to the weighmaster's window. The tears I'd shed had mixed with the dirt on my face, leaving a trail of streaks and no way to hide them.

"Uh, you OK, man?" he mumbled.

"I am," I said. "I'm feeling a lot lighter now."

And the truth is, I really was.

Reflection Questions

1. Does something specific come to mind when you think about where you need to forgive yourself? What prevents you from taking that step?

2. What is your perspective on forgiveness? How has it changed as you've experienced grief?

3. Share about a time in your life when you've let go of your anger and experienced the lightness Steve mentioned in this chapter. What was that like for you?

CHAPTER 9

SAVING FERRIS

Will You Still Love Me in the Morning?

What happens when your ego is served a death blow? Let's say your pride takes the kind of hit you have no hope of recovering from. What do you do when the entire world you've been waiting for, preparing for, and fighting for comes crashing down? I'm pretty sure what usually follows is a massive identity crisis. That's what I experienced after leaving Willow. I went from being the person stepping into one of the most influential and highly regarded church leadership roles to being the man resigning in protest and moving away to a town where nobody knew him.

I remember not long after our move to Arizona, I returned to the townhouse my family was renting to meet a Home Depot delivery guy who was bringing us a new washer and dryer. As he arrived, I felt the urge to explain why I was home at 10:30 a.m. on a Wednesday. In my old life, back at Willow, my days had been full. I knew what to expect, and I had a routine I could count on. But when we experience loss, our routines get disrupted, and we feel the absence immensely. I didn't know what to do with my days now that I wasn't building and dreaming alongside my coworkers at Willow and was just beginning to get speaking engagements on my own. Instead of packed schedules and busy meetings, I found myself standing in my house feeling guilty and embarrassed to be home on a weekday.

As I signed the receipts for the appliances, an inner voice was urging me to explain to the delivery guy why I was home. When someone used to ask me what I did for work, I had a title and a position and a place of employment to point to. Now I had nothing. I realized I wanted to impress this deliveryman with all the thousands of people I used to speak to weekly and all the world leaders and influencers I've met and talked with. I was afraid that if I didn't, he would judge me as a slacker nobody. This internal dialogue grossed me out, but it was real. I didn't say anything to him, but as soon as he left, I grabbed my journal and started taking notes. What was going on in my heart? Why did I suddenly want to justify my circumstances? Why did I want to defend my work ethic and past accomplishments? Take away the stage, congregation, title, and role, and who am I?

Right after I resigned from Willow, I received offers to work elsewhere. Some churches and nonprofits wanted me to work for them, to continue doing what I'd been doing at Willow. It would have been an easy choice, a no-brainer, if you will. But I was wounded and needed healing before I had any business leading others again. I couldn't see straight and had no sense which way was up anymore, so to have stepped directly into another pastoral role would have been selfish and dangerous not only to myself but to the congregation I'd have been entrusted to lead.

Instead, I could travel on the weekends to speak at churches, and that would be enough to keep my family afloat while protecting us from the pressure of leading a church while we healed. So that's what I did. I continued the work of teaching the Bible and connecting with people, only I was jumping on planes to do so.

This desert detox brought to the surface all the ways my role at Willow had allowed me to avoid specific questions. This is the thing about grief that few talk about—it unravels us as we untangle it, *and* we find ourselves grieving the loss over what we thought it would be. We mourn our preferred future *and* our separation all at once.

Part of honoring what comes up when change happens is wrestling with how we thought it would be.

Maybe you thought Dad would walk you down the aisle, but he is no longer with you.

Perhaps you thought Mom would be present for the birth of your first, but she is too sick to come.

Maybe you expected that friend to stand at your wedding, but now you don't speak to each other.

You thought it would be one thing. You were so confident you knew how it would go. And then life does what life does, and you realize that person won't be there to witness your most significant experiences ever again.

Grief is us saying, "It's not supposed to be like this."

But it's even more than that.

It's also the untangling that we each must do as we grieve. My therapist reminds me often that betrayal is a valid and natural form of trauma. When some breach of trust and safety occurs, we are harmed and traumatized emotionally just as if we'd been hurt or harmed physically. It is all a form of violation and lack of consent and manipulation.

When we've experienced betrayal trauma, we wonder what was true and what wasn't. We compare our perception of reality with what happened, the two becoming confusing and muddy. Gaslighting is a standard tool used in betrayal trauma cases. We wonder, *When they said that, what did they mean?* And, *I took their words at face value, but was their response intended to protect themselves from me getting closer to the truth?*

As I regained my bearings under the hot Phoenix sun, I realized I had some misaligned issues regarding my ego. And to be honest, I was terrified of what God would have to do to help me calibrate and get myself right again. For some reason, that journey began with a man named Zacchaeus.

One day, as Jesus walked the eighteen-mile dusty trail from Jericho to Jerusalem, crowds began to form around him.

At one point, Jesus looked up to see a man who had climbed into a tree and appeared to be enthralled with every word he spoke. From Luke 19, we learn a few interesting facts about this tree climber: He was a chief tax collector who was extremely wealthy. His name was Zacchaeus, which means "pure" or "untainted." But in the eyes of every Jewish person surrounding Jesus, Zacchaeus was deeply tainted. The Roman government had contracted him to gather income taxes from specific districts of the Roman Empire. Backed by the most potent military force of the day, Zacchaeus extorted hardworking Jews by levying taxes on their households. Zacchaeus kept some of the bounty for himself and gave the rest to the empire. This was his job. It's what he did every day:

Take money.

Extort.

Provide for the empire.

Repeat.

Zacchaeus became very rich in this system as he watched the poor get poorer. He was hated. He was despised. He was considered treasonous by the Jewish people. But he had money. A lot of it. He had no real friends, but he had security guards. I can imagine his loneliness, a deep-rooted lack of satisfaction in his soul. As Zacchaeus sat in the tree, he heard the Rabbi call him by name: "Zacchaeus, hurry down. Today is my day to be a guest in your home" (Luke 19:5 MSG).

Zacchaeus couldn't believe it. Did somebody *that* important want to stay at his house? Not just anybody, but a rabbi? Even the crowds began questioning Jesus' motives, asking,

"What business does he have getting cozy with this crook?" (v. 7 MSG). Scholars say twelve thousand priests lived in Jericho and took turns traveling to Jerusalem to serve at the temple.[1] So there wasn't a shortage of "holy" people Jesus could have stayed with. But Jesus didn't care. He saw someone who longed to embody the meaning of his name. He saw someone who wanted to go from impure to pure again, from tainted to untainted. So Jesus invited himself over.

Before the Rabbi and tax collector broke from the crowd, Zacchaeus proclaimed, "Master, I give away half my income to the poor—and if I'm caught cheating, I pay four times the damages" (v. 8 MSG).

Jesus quickly remarked, "Today is salvation day in this home! Here he is: Zacchaeus, son of Abraham! For the Son of Man came to find and restore the lost" (vv. 9–10 MSG).

This is one of Scripture's most moving salvation stories for me. We don't just see someone encountering Jesus, but salvation breaks forth, and the response from his heart is to give back to the poor.

But here's the question: What happened the next day? Did Zacchaeus go back to work for the Roman Empire? Did the now-pure one go back to being impure?

With Jericho as a backdrop and the city of Jerusalem in his view, Jesus went on to tell the parable of the ten minas (Luke 19:11–27), which is often misinterpreted and confused with the legend of talents. But they are two wildly different parables.

The parable of the ten minas is about what Zacchaeus will do tomorrow.

Jesus infused culture into his storytelling when he started the parable, detailing that "a man of noble birth went to a distant country to have himself appointed king and then to return. So he called ten of his servants and gave them ten minas. 'Put this money to work,' he said, 'until I come back.' But his subjects hated him and sent a delegation after him to say, 'We don't want this man to be our king'" (vv. 12–14).

The Jewish historian Josephus recounted that King Herod's son, Archelaus, went to Rome to be appointed king and that a delegation paid their way to Rome to oppose this decision. This delegation couldn't stand Herod's empire continuing, primarily because Archelaus was known to be just as bloodthirsty. Where did Archelaus live? He restored his father's palace, which he named Archelaus, right outside Jericho.

So Jesus was telling a parable of a bloodthirsty leader who wants to be king and needs his workers to make him money to look good for the empire.

This is the system Zacchaeus worked in.

In Jesus' parable, the king calls for the servants he had given money to: "The first one came and said, 'Sir, your mina has earned ten more.' 'Well done, my good servant!' his master replied. 'Because you have been trustworthy in a very small matter, take charge of ten cities'" (vv. 16–17). In other words, the king was saying, "Way to take money, extort, and provide more income for the empire! You deserve ten more cities to do the same thing."

Jesus continued, "The second came and said, 'Sir, your mina has earned five more.' His master answered, 'You take charge of five cities'" (vv. 18–19). The second servant also received praise from the king for his cunning and extortion.

"Then another servant came and said, 'Sir, here is your mina; I have kept it laid away in a piece of cloth. I was afraid of you, because you are a hard man. You take out what you did not put in and reap what you did not sow'" (vv. 20–21).

This was who Zacchaeus would be the next day he went to work. He would take the money he received and do nothing with it. No more making money. No more extorting. No more providing for the empire. It would be a total regime change.

In Jesus' parable, the master lashes out at this servant, takes the mina away, and gives it to the most profitable servant, who already has ten (vv. 22–24).

Jesus understood what the next week would bring. As he prepared to enter Jerusalem, he would be cheered, denied, betrayed, mocked, tried, beaten, and crucified. Jesus understood the empire's power. This wasn't some nice story he was trying to tell Zacchaeus. He was helping him understand this: "Zacchaeus, for too long you were willfully blind to what this system did to those around you. The ways they took, stole, extorted, punished, and hurt good people. You can't return to that. Even though you are good at it, it's tainting your soul. There's more for you in my Father's kingdom, but it will look much different than what you are accustomed to."

Jesus' parable ends with another historical reminder of the corrupt system when it details how Archelaus gathers all those who had come to Rome to oppose his being king, and he has them killed right before him (vv. 26–27).

We don't know from Scripture if Zacchaeus returned to working for the empire or chose to step into the kingdom of God and live as a disciple of Jesus. Zacchaeus had everything to lose.

But here's the thing: once you see, it's hard to unsee.

Many of us work hard not to see what might be obvious. We choose willful blindness, preferring to stay naive or purposely looking the other way. Zacchaeus had heard the story of someone who decided to no longer work for the empire. All he had known was to make, extort, and provide for the empire. What would he do now? Would he give it all up for some Jewish rabbi? Or would he stay willfully blind and silence his inner screams of dissatisfaction?

The same questions apply to us. Will we choose to be tainted but at least benefit from wrongdoing? Or will we choose instead to be pure and live by faith?

When Jesus called his disciples, the Scriptures tell us he simply said, "*Lech aharai*," which translated from Hebrew means "walk after me."[2] If you're like me, it's easy to become distracted by responsibilities, to-do lists, responding to emails, and worrying about tomorrow. These can all be done with good intentions. However, we can miss walking after Jesus. Remember how simple his invitation has always been: "*Lech aharai*, my friend." Walk after him. Only him.

When salvation comes to your house, it begins a total regime change. Your allegiance is to the cross, your citizenship is in heaven, your loyalty is to Christ alone, the invitation is *lech aharai*, and your anthem is, "I am an Easter person living in a Good Friday world."

We can't stay silent anymore.

We can't choose willful blindness any longer.

We must simply follow him.

No matter what the cost.

No matter where it leads.

The fact is, Zacchaeus, you, and I are replaceable. The Roman Empire will find another person to take our spots, to be willfully blind and continue to take, extort, and provide for the empire.

While I was living in the desert, one of the highlights for me was creating the *Home Team* podcast with Sam Acho and Sam Ponder. It was a space for us to chop it up about the unique intersection of faith, sports, and culture. I'll never forget when Sam Ponder shared that one of the truths every ESPN anchorperson knows is this: "Everyone is replaceable."[3]

Hearing her say those words, I was speechless. Sam Ponder can't be replaceable. She hosts *NFL Countdown*, the premier NFL pregame show. Sam Acho, an NFL player for the Chicago Bears, reiterated her comments by saying, "There are only so many spots on an NFL roster, and in every draft, there is someone younger who wants your job. Everyone is replaceable."

Zacchaeus was replaceable.

Sam Ponder is replaceable.

Sam Acho is replaceable.

Steve Carter is replaceable.

The machine will continue. The empire will find a replacement. The business will continue to serve the bottom line. And at that moment, we finally grasp the earth-shattering reality that it's not enough to be loyal or talented. The establishment can still choose to move on with someone new. This is why the healthiest versions of ourselves must be deeply rooted in our belovedness, not in what we do, how much we make, who we are with, or what title we carry for a larger institution.

My time in the desert helped me realize how intricately my value and meaning were tied with my career. I became more aware of my codependency issues and began to get a better assessment of the work I had ahead of me in order to heal. Whenever I was introduced as the "former lead teaching pastor at Willow Creek," it silently triggered me. It felt like someone was unintentionally (or maybe intentionally) saying my best days were behind me. But now I can view that introduction differently, knowing my time at Willow was a season that shaped me significantly and helped me uncover the values that truly drive me. It was a time in which I finally began to realize how the issues of workaholism, codependency, people-pleasing, and image management were holding me back from following after Christ.

Once during a Sunday service at Willow, I had the chance to interview US gymnast Simone Biles. Backstage, she was as cheerful and delightful as you could imagine. She was gracious and patient, indulging various staff members and our families in selfies and stories from her illustrious career as a gymnast. Her weekend interview drew more people than Willow usually experienced—the second-highest-attended weekend ever. I had such a ball getting to learn from her. One statement she made has stuck with me all this time. It was the moment when she said, "I'm not trying to be anyone else. I'm trying to be the first Simone Biles."[4]

She stood on that stage as the most decorated US gymnast and arguably the most outstanding female gymnast of all time, reminding us that our most important work is to be our whole selves. She was an advocate and an ally to those, including herself, who had come forward to report abuse. She showed courage by choosing to remove herself from the Olympics when she was struggling. She wasn't trying to impress anyone or be someone she was not.

Athletes, celebrities, leaders, and pastors sometimes struggle to prioritize their mental, emotional, and spiritual health. They're hanging on, trying to eke out one more year, one more chance to perform. It's because they need it more than it needs them.

Zacchaeus needed the Roman Empire more than the empire needed him.

I needed Willow more than Willow needed me.

Sitting with that reality—that I was replaceable, that I wasn't that important, that the show would go on—was both profoundly challenging and an invitation to heal.

Luke 19 doesn't end with Jesus' parable but with Palm Sunday. It's as if Jesus were saying there are two kingdoms: one empire was centered on fear (the king will kill those who oppose, and replace those who don't follow the company line), and the other kingdom is centered on unconditional love (the king will die for those who fight, and empower anyone willing to join him in carrying the cross on behalf of another).

For much of my life, I was following Jesus, but I wanted to be like Ferris Bueller, the iconic 1980s movie character. I wanted to be needed. I wanted to be liked. I tried to connect what someone needed with the person or organization who could help them. I tried so hard to make everyone around me feel so great that I didn't know what it meant to experience someone not liking, respecting, or appreciating me (at least to my face). But the realization that I was replaceable was ultimately good for my ego and helped me face my codependent tendencies. I needed to recenter my identity on being Christ's beloved, even when others didn't feel that way.

It is like good soup for the soul, admitting we are sick and need to get well. We're hiding the mina, not playing the game or manipulating someone's trust.

It was as if Jesus was saying to me during that time, *Listen, Steve. You have some choices to make. I'm not saying Ferris isn't a cool guy. Hey, we're a lot alike. But that's not really what we're talking about here. You need to examine your motivation, not your attributes.*

Oof. I had been trying so hard to be *the right kind of guy* when God wanted me to live with *the right motivation.* Instead of a motivation to get ahead, to secure my place and value within a team or organization, I needed to embrace the truth that God loves me just as I am. Instead of trying to make people feel better so they would like me, I needed to love them and see them purely as God does. Not because I needed something from them but because they, too, are God's beloved.

I was replaceable, *and that's OK.*

I needed to be needed, *and that's OK.*

I wanted to be wanted, *and that's OK.*

I am not Ferris Bueller, *and that's OK.*

The truth is, we have to die to those unhealthy motivations before we can start embracing who we truly are. For me, my ego fought and clawed to stick around as I walked along those desert trails. But my eyes were already refocusing on something more beautiful: Jesus. I was becoming ready to lay it all down at his feet for the chance to live more and more in alignment with who he saw me to be: myself. I wonder, my friend, what it might feel like for you to live in more alignment with your truest self. I imagine you would feel more free, more clear, and more hopeful as well. This is the continuation of our GBR Journey as we keep trusting the process as we learn to trust ourselves.

Reflection Questions

1. Take some time to write down some of your motivations and allow God to show you where they might be helping or hindering your grief journey.

2. Have you ever been in a situation where you felt like you had something to prove during a season of loss? What was that experience like?

3. What is one way you can try to live more in alignment with the principles of Jesus this week?

CHAPTER 10

CROSS + RELEASE

How Heavy Is Your Backpack?

An ancient trail known as the Camino de Santiago winds
and turns through France, Portugal, and Spain. People
from all over the world come to walk its dusty roads. Most of
them are in search of something. I was invited to join a group
setting out to hike the Camino the month I turned forty-
three. It was a bucket-list item, so I jumped at the opportunity.
However, this hike isn't something you do lightly. From the
months of preparation, the hundreds of miles I spent training, to the monthly Zoom check-ins with the group traveling,
this trip was brimming with intention. We were committed

to honesty and dedication to our diets, training, integrity, and inner selves. We were all coming to the trail with a question, hope, prayer, and quest.

As I prepped for my Camino experience, I did a ton of research on what to bring. *What essentials should I include in my pack before embarking on this adventure?* I expected a hefty REI bill in my future as I pictured towering piles of sleeping bags, lamps, heaters, bug spray, tents, utensils, and more. To my surprise, the veterans who had braved the trail told us a different story. "Travel lightly" was a common answer. "You won't need nearly as much as you think you will." I struggled to believe this was true as I thought of all we'd encounter.

On the eve of my pilgrimage, I nervously began to fill my backpack. Surely I would need a sleeping bag, a pillow, extra clothes, and socks. I should also bring a few different jackets because I didn't know how cold it would get at night. I threw in some extra toiletries, a water bottle, a journal, a couple of books, and many snacks. Oh, those hiking poles should definitely come with me too. I'm sure you can imagine how the next part went. I must have tried for over half an hour to cram all the items into my backpack. I took everything out and put it back in, changing the order and reorganizing repeatedly. No matter how I did it, the zipper simply would not be moved. But how could I get through this challenge without all these things? Everything felt vital, and I was convinced I couldn't part with any of it. I finally gave up, heaving and red-faced, and walked down the stairs to join my bewildered family for dinner.

"Dad? What were you doing up there?" my daughter asked. I laughed as I imagined what all my stomping and sorting must have sounded like from downstairs.

"I was in a war with a backpack," I replied. After a pause, I admitted, "The backpack won."

My wife started giggling, trying to hide the laugh, making it even more hilarious. Before long, we were all in hysterics. Backpack: 1, Steve: 0.

Later, after the kids were in bed, I returned to my opponent, the Osprey Exos 58. It was still splayed out on the floor where I'd left it. Half-zipped, its contents spilled all over the carpet. I had to look at each item critically and decide how crucial it was for the journey ahead. I pulled each piece out again, and one by one, I asked, "Is this really essential?" For every no, I set the item aside. Perhaps I wouldn't really need those hiking poles, and I guess fourteen pairs of heavy-duty socks might be overkill. Slowly, the yes pile shrank. I tried one more time to load that backpack, and to my relief, it zipped. Victory!

Except that, as I pulled the beast from the ground and attempted to slide its straps over my shoulders, I could tell there was no way I could hike over a hundred miles with it on my back. My shoulders were already starting to ache, and my lower back was throbbing. It weighed way too much.

Just because it fit didn't mean it was essential.

The words of the wise, seasoned hikers I'd read in those online forums echoed in my mind: *You don't need as much as you think you do.* I put down my backpack and did another edit, removing more items. Slowly but surely, I got that pack down to the perfect balance of need and comfort.

When the day finally arrived to embark on my Camino pilgrimage, I loaded my backpack in the back of an Uber and headed to the airport. It was hard to believe I would have all I'd need in that little pack, yet I knew there was no way I could bring one more thing. At a certain point, I had to trust that I had enough.

As I walked into the airport, feeling the reality of all I was literally carrying on my back, I couldn't help but think of all the weightiness I'd been carrying around for a long, long time. My back had been aching under the emotional weight of disappointment, betrayal, loss, and grief, and I'd just kept adding more and more to the pack. Piling it all on, forcing myself to keep going, ignoring the signals of pain my body had been sending, refusing to let go of any of the past, insisting I could handle it all.

My body had been carrying so much for so long.

A friend of mine who is a therapist once told me, "Eighty percent of my clients come to me because they are struggling to forgive someone. If people could learn to forgive independently, I would be out of a job."

I wouldn't have thought I had a forgiveness problem when he told me that. I liked to think of myself as someone who had grace and didn't hold on to the past. But as I stood in line to grab my seat on the plane, I realized I had a lot of internal baggage to sort out. Suddenly, the plans and expectations I'd had for what I thought I'd be processing on the Camino went out the window, and it became clear I had a lot of pent-up past pain to unravel.

In the ancient texts, we encounter a God familiar with forgiveness. In the Hebrew scriptures, we meet a God who understood how potent shame was within humanity. Story after story showcases another facet of shame. Whether it manifested as worry, anxiety, codependence, control, deceit, or hatred, the roots found themselves in the ethos of shame. Shame has the power to co-opt the good within someone.

I'm about to introduce an old word and attempt to give it a new meaning for us. But you've got to promise you'll stay with me and try to keep an open mind. OK? Here we go.

What is *sin*? This word has too often been weaponized against the marginalized and poor for thousands of years by religious communities and people in spaces of power and privilege. They still use this word to invoke shame and keep people afraid and unwilling to rise up. The message is this: *you have done wrong and need me (or what I can give you) to make it right.*

However, the true intent of sin is to live less than what is possible for you. Essentially, we sin when we self-sabotage, when we don't live up to our fullest potential, our fullest selves, our truest and best form of humanity. To fall short of what God wants for us is to sin.

Now, that seems like an impossible task, doesn't it? No one is perfect, after all. These ancient texts tell the story of a God interacting with humanity. They account for the divine's attempt at a relationship with their creation. Whenever we sin against ourselves, we choose something less than God's desire for us; whenever we sin against another, we choose something less than God's desire for them.

Once a year, the Jewish community celebrates what is commonly referred to as the holiest day of the year, the Day of Atonement. The festival is known as Yom Kippur, and in ancient times, the nation of Israel would put the sins of the people onto a goat that would be released and sent away into the wild (Leviticus 16:21–22). This was a visual, tactile picture of each sin being sent far away from the community. In the Lord's Prayer, Jesus said that heaven will invade earth when we forgive the debts of another (Matthew 6:9–13). The Greek word translated as "forgive" is *aphiemi*; it has its roots in Yom Kippur, which means to release and send it away.[1]

On the plane to Portugal, I took out my journal and started to write more about the realization I'd had about my own grief and lack of forgiveness. As I wrote, I remembered specific moments and stories. I jotted each one down, the words coming faster than my pen would allow. One after the other, past grievances and frustrations came to mind. I remembered conversations I'd completely forgotten about. I replayed old memories of things that had been said, or left unsaid, and let myself feel some anger and sadness all over again.

Do you know what's really wild? The people responsible for our wounds rarely think about us. They aren't weighed down with grief. They aren't burdened with anger. They aren't walking around with a two-hundred-pound backpack full of pain on their backs. They continue to move on with their lives while we get left holding the bag.

Not having to carry around a massive load of unresolved pain might be reason enough to work on forgiving, but there's another worthy benefit, and it has to do with your physical health. Research shows that being unable to forgive fosters anger, hostility, and stress, which are well-documented to impact mental and physical health.[2] Many doctors are beginning to connect the dots between unforgiveness and serious diseases. "There is an enormous physical burden to being hurt and disappointed," said Karen Swartz, MD, director of the Mood Disorders Adult Consultation Clinic at Johns Hopkins Hospital.[3]

Whether it's due to a spat with a friend or spouse, or something that strikes deeper, unforgiveness takes its toll. When you have all that toxicity and negativity flowing within, how can it not have an effect on your body and your well-being?

In the Bible, the apostle Paul used another word for forgiveness (Ephesians 4:32). He preferred *charizomai*, which I like to define as "the grace you received you freely give away."[4] This grace is the atonement Paul believed was given to us by the death of Jesus, who he considered Christ. It's as if Paul understood that the spiritual act of forgiveness would always bring us back to the foot of the cross. Being a Christian myself, this perspective is incredibly beautiful to me. *Charizomai* brings me back to the small wooden cross I carry in my pocket. I mentioned earlier that I've carried a small wooden cross in my pocket for the past few years. It serves as a reminder of the grace I've received and to make the choice to offer it freely. I have the choice to give it away fully. Or not.

As I think of the weighty, proverbial backpack of pain, I can safely say that I hadn't freely given grace away for most of my life. If I'm honest, I used my anger as fuel. I gained energy from it—negative, toxic, and dangerous energy. All that pressure affected my emotional, physical, mental, and spiritual well-being. This is why I believe God gave us the ability to choose forgiveness. Maybe it was so that we could use our free will to release the past and walk with more freedom, peace, grace, and love into our present and future.

What I've come to realize is that forgiveness is a solo sport. Forgiveness is an act you must freely choose to do. No one can force you; you can't forgive yourself before you're ready. You can be free only after you are sick and tired of carrying that extra dead weight. Forgiveness is a process. It takes time. The deeper the pain you've experienced, the more complex the healing and, therefore, the longer and more difficult the practice of forgiveness tends to be.

Most of my anger at that time revolved around betrayal. The career I'd put my life into preparing for was sabotaged by the betrayal of people I trusted and looked up to. What I thought would be the crowning achievement of my professional life came crashing down as the scandal of sexual misconduct by my former boss and the subsequent decades of leadership cover-up became public. If that wasn't enough, they wanted me to participate in the cover-up. They wanted me to lie to the church community and interviewers.

Remembering the moment I confronted my rage back at the cohort, when I took all that energy out on pillows while others bore witness, I suddenly realized that while I had processed the anger, I hadn't actually done any forgiving. I was still in a prison of my making, and until that moment on the plane, I couldn't find a way to lay my burdens down.

I put my hand in my pocket, grabbed that small carved cross, and inhaled and exhaled a few times. Two Greek words for "forgiveness," *charizomai* and *aphiemi,* came to mind. *Come to the foot of the cross and let it go.*

I shut my eyes and whispered a small prayer under my breath: "Cross + release + send it away."

When we sense unforgiveness, *cross + release + send it away.*

When we get hung up on a weighty grievance we haven't had the courage to face, *cross + release + send it away.*

When we can't bear the weight of the emotional baggage we've been carrying, *cross + release + send it away.*

We reflect on the memory that is most poignant and present in our mind, and we picture bringing it to the foot of the cross. Then we let go, releasing it and sending it far away. Forgiveness doesn't require an apology from the one who wronged us. Most of the time, an apology will never come. But we can still choose to forgive and move forward with our lives, free from bitterness. Forgiveness is a solo sport, but we each have a chance to play.

Reflection Questions

1. What have you been carrying in your backpack that needs to be taken out?

2. Is there a place in your journey where you have felt lost? What was that like? What did you learn from that experience?

3. Take time and reflect on one person you have not forgiven. What needs to happen for you to be able to release them and move on?

CHAPTER 11

FOUND AND LOST

What's Your Call Sign?

When I was hiking the Camino de Santiago, I loved getting up early while it was still dark out. I'd brush my teeth, wash my face, put on two pairs of socks, grab my backpack, and head out for the trek. Most mornings, I saw the sunrise as I'd walk for a few hours and then stop at a café, grab a cup of coffee and chocolate croissant, pull out my journal, read from my little black Bible, and start to write as the townspeople began their day.

There's something about a pilgrimage that brings up the things beneath the thing you've been holding on to for way too long. To pilgrimage is a sacred practice, one that people in the ancient Near East would often do to head to the temple for the various festivals. The subtle beat of walking—right leg, left leg, right step, left step—is comforting. In many ways, this sacred practice has been forgotten. Still, we're beginning to see a resurgence as people hike Machu Picchu, the Appalachian Trail, and various mountains around the globe, or retrace the steps of leaders like Saint James on the Camino de Santiago.

When it was all said and done, the trail I took was over one hundred miles. I'd never walked that much in my life! I'd gone on some epic trips but never a pilgrimage like that.

When we began meeting monthly to prepare for this pilgrimage, my friends Jon and Mark kept telling us that the Camino starts when you decide to go on this journey and will continue long after you finish the trail. That's the spiritual power of a pilgrimage.

In some of my readings of the Desert Fathers and Mothers, I came across this quote: "You need a spiritual pilgrimage. Begin by closing your mouth."[1] I thought about this while I was hiking the trails of Arizona, and it came to mind often while I was trekking the Camino.

Begin by closing your mouth. Just listen. Make room for quiet. No distractions. Pay attention to what is stirring within and around you. Hold space for what peeks out from within. The more your body trusts that you are safe, the more it will feel comfortable bringing up thoughts and feelings it's been harboring. That's the power of pilgrimage—you are creating a safe space within yourself.

One morning as I was walking in Portugal, I got lost in processing all the weight and sorrow I was still carrying. Shortly after I resigned from Willow, someone from the church who had been my friend asked to meet with me. I wasn't sure what to expect from our time together, but the meeting was harder than I had anticipated. The sadness and anger were palpable. I wasn't emotionally prepared for what he told me: "Whenever someone leaves a meeting or event early, people often say, 'Don't Carter me.'"

Don't leave me.

Don't abandon me.

Don't be like Carter.

The statement was cruel, heartless, and mean. I felt misunderstood and trivialized all at once. I felt embarrassed and hurt that my decision to leave Willow, resigning in protest and in support of the victims, would be used in such a careless way. Long after that meeting ended, I couldn't get the thought out of my head. Whenever the phrase came to mind, it would siphon all my energy, leaving me mentally drained for the rest of the day. I wondered who had said it. I wondered if anyone had laughed when it was first mentioned. It hurt when I imagined my former coworkers smirking and nodding when they heard it. I tried to play it off for a while, saying that it didn't pull or stick to my heart, but it definitely did.

During my pilgrimage to Camino, I realized that it's often the people with whom we feel the safest that we let see our most authentic selves. After Bill retired early from Willow amid the scandal, he left social media and didn't make any public appearances. He essentially became publicly inaccessible.

I, on the other hand, didn't have any savings or a fall-back plan, and my work required that I travel and spend time speaking publicly. I was accessible. I was available. I was out there for people to find and point to. And maybe, to hate and make fun of and laugh at.

People could get to me, and so could their words. Sure, their anger wasn't always about me, but they could throw darts, and I would engage. They couldn't reach the founder or his enablers, but I gave them access and an outlet. I didn't know how to hold so much heavy emotion of my own, let alone that of others. Somehow, I had been absorbing it. And much like the backpack that had been too heavy to travel with, all that weight was proving too much for me to hold inside. It was eating me alive. I realized there was another way to look at this. I could translate what someone inferred with a higher sense of reality. When someone took their anger out on me, I could translate it to mean, "I don't know what to do with my grief. I don't want to hold it anymore, so I'm giving it to you."

It took the edge off when I reframed it that way. It made what they were saying less personal. It didn't make it right, but it proved that many people didn't know how to grieve. And honestly, neither did I. I took out my pen and wrote down some of the phrases I had heard people say or seen posted online about me. I put my hand over my heart and read each painful statement. I inhaled and exhaled. Then I translated it and transferred it to who it was really meant for.

"You are such a coward" translated to, *Our expectation was that you would be here with us; this wasn't your fault; we wish you didn't have to go.*

"You couldn't hack it as the leader anyway" translated to, *I can't even begin to imagine the place you were in, one you should never have had to be in. We can get through this together.*

"I'm so mad at you" translated to, *Bill was my pastor, and Willow was my safe place. When you left, it all fell apart, and I feel hopeless now.*

And on and on.

It was like pulling back the Band-Aid, letting in some oxygen, and cleaning the wound with peroxide. It burned as I wrote out each phrase, but I knew this process was also relieving the pain that was at risk of being infected with bitterness and resentment that wasn't mine to hold. For the first time since hearing that phrase, "Don't Carter me," I felt like I could exhale.

My counselor has taught me the power of "meaning-making." Stories, words, or experiences will stick to us, and if we're not careful, we will give them a meaning that isn't true. The more challenging work is to look at the grief, look at those phrases, acknowledge the weight and pain they caused, and give them a proper meaning. That is what this practice did for me. It helped me to interpret correctly, translate and transfer what was not for me, and breathe again. This meaning-making process became a gift for my heart, mind, body, and soul.

I wiped my eyes and continued on the Camino de Santiago trail, following the yellow arrows to the next town.

As I walked some more, processing my grief, I missed my turn. It wasn't until I walked on a bridge that went over a freeway that I realized how far I'd gotten from the trail. With my backpack and walking stick, I started to look around to get my bearings and figure out how to get some help back to where I was supposed to be. Cars were zooming below, and I couldn't see another person in any direction. For the first time since embarking on this hike, I was alone. I had no cell reception and no way of telling where I was. *I was lost.*

Those three words were something I had never wanted to be. As someone who relentlessly set goals, worked to achieve them, and knew the next strategic play, I realized I had felt profoundly lost these past few years.

Lost.

In Luke 15, Jesus told three stories about being lost after religious leaders questioned him for eating with people they considered "less than." He told a story of a sheep lost outside a house, a coin lost inside a home, and a tale of two lost siblings and a father who greets them both with equal love.

Three stories all about being lost. The central point of all these stories is this: you can be lost outside the house, and you can be lost inside the house. Regardless, the Father celebrates whenever lost things are found.

What was Jesus doing with these stories? He was inviting the religious people who had the gall to question his decision to eat with whomever he wanted to consider that their faith might not be big enough or wide enough for the kingdom he was ushering forth. "It's different than you think," he was telling them. "The people you call 'less than' aren't the only ones lost here. You are lost too." It was a giant invitation to experience the goodness of grace, peace, and acceptance that comes from being found by Christ and by sharing a faith far more expansive than they dared to imagine.

When presented with this kind of invitation, many religious leaders, past and present, during Jesus' day and today, rely more on what they can control and measure over where the Spirit is leading and guiding. It's a guise we all tend to use at some point in our lives, to protect ourselves from feeling lost and out of control. We all *know* we aren't immortal, but most of us grapple with our mortality. We don't want to face the death of what we thought our lives would look, be, and feel like. No one wants to suffer. This is why most of us have, on occasion, worked to curate our lives in a way meant to protect ourselves from pain, disappointment, uncertainty, and feeling out of control. When religious communities focus only on the good, the positive, and the spin, they miss a massive part of what it is to minister to humanity.

It makes sense that so many people are deconstructing matters of faith. One massive reason may be that they haven't been able to bring their doubts, questions, and experiences of being out of control to their pastors without being told something trite like "God is in control" or "Just pray about it." As we encounter more of the knocks of life, our simple faith statements sometimes don't hold water, and we have nowhere to bring our bigger theological questions within our churches. It hasn't been safe to do so. I've always desired a strong faith to hold all my doubts, fears, and questions, where I wonder and wrestle with theology and all the parts of me that are still lost and in process.

It's just easier said than done.

Back on that highway overpass in Portugal, I admitted to myself that I was lost in more ways than one. I had to realize how out of control my life had felt and how unsure I was of what was actually next for me to do in this life.

I screamed out on that bridge, "Lord, I'm lost! Please help me!"

A few minutes later, a lady driving in the other direction began to slow down. She must have seen my backpack and how far from the trail I was. She slowed to a stop on the side of the road, rolled down her window, and yelled, "Are you looking for the Camino?"

I laughed and replied, "Yes!"

She stuck her head out the window and pointed to where I needed to go to get back on the trail. I thanked her profusely and headed toward the trailhead. Cutting through a bunch of brush and trees, I returned to the familiar place of yellow arrows that reminded me I was on the right path. That night, as the group was debriefing, I spoke about getting lost, the deep feelings of fear I'd carried within about getting lost, and the reality that I *am* lost. It was the first time I had ever admitted that to anyone. Without missing a beat, my friend Jon replied, "If you never get lost, you can never be found."

In most church settings, we talk about the lost being found as a reference to someone being saved by accepting

Jesus and being baptized, but I was beginning to wonder if there might be another way to think about being lost. What if Jesus was teaching us that his kingdom is open to anyone who feels lost?

Lost in faith.

Lost in the future.

Lost in grief.

We can't be found if we never admit we're lost. Yet the good news is that when we accept we're lost, we give ourselves the best chance of being found again. Someone, somewhere, will hear our woeful and desperate cries for help, and they will slow down and point us back to the path we're searching for.

Many weekend services are designed to lift spirits and make attendees feel hope, joy, and celebration. There is nothing wrong with wanting to go to church to feel better. Joy and celebration are beautiful parts of faith and humanity. But they are not the whole story, and when we don't make room for the whole story, we miss out on a lot.

Many religious spaces within Christianity have neglected to teach people what to do with their grief, lament, repentance, and feelings of loss. Many churches delegate conversations and teachings on grief and lament to a weekday class or book study. Many pastors only mention race on Martin Luther King Jr. Day. My friend Jenny calls these services "skim MiLK." We all do this to a certain extent. You see it often on social media. A tragedy is announced, and people change their profile pictures, post black squares, and hashtag in solidarity. And then a week or two later, it's all back to how it was before.

Yet in the Bible, an entire book called Lamentations and forty-two psalms are dedicated to lament. Most Christians, especially in the United States, don't know how to lament, grieve, and sit uncomfortably very well. Why is this? By only talking about grief on Good Friday, churches communicate that there isn't room for grief on the other 364 days of the year. It sends an unspoken message that your messy life doesn't belong in the sanctuary. Good vibes only. Leave your sadness at the door. Many people attempt to do this and can for a while. But one way or another, each of us will encounter disruption that causes us to fall to our knees, lost and alone. What do we do then?

One of my favorite quotes comes from the tombstone of Ruth Bell Graham, which says, "End of construction—Thank you for your patience."[2] Isn't that stunning? The sentiment is so theologically rich as she beautifully unpacks that none of us ever fully arrive this side of heaven. Are we saved? Yes! But are there areas where we can still go deeper with Jesus to discover more of God's heartbeat for humanity? Of course!

What I began to discover is that even though I am found in Christ, saved and forever a child of God, I am also a work in progress. I will always have more to learn, more invitations to expand, more chances to learn better and do better. We all will. Where the pulpit offered feel-good messaging, I was hungry for something more, something I could hold on to through the dark night of my soul.

Over the decades as I've had the privilege to pastor community members in churches from California to Chile to

Chicago and more, I realized very quickly that those bumper-sticker platitudes didn't hold up when sitting across from a grieving widow whose husband of more than fifty years had just passed away. They didn't provide guidance for the teenager whose older sibling died by suicide. I've sat with countless people as they shared their deep pain and wondered, *What can I possibly say to help them feel better?* Our grief muscles are weak when we don't regularly engage them. It was only by embracing what I did not know and learning by bearing witness to another's grief that I was able to begin using that muscle more.

I still have so many areas where the Holy Spirit is at work in me. Some days I can feel quite overwhelmed as I sit in Scripture and ask God to show me how I can better embody the tenets of grief. The life of Jesus has continued to be a beacon of inspiration for me. He was always calling his disciples closer to the heart of God. *Be more still. Be more honest. Be less afraid. Be present in your life.* The fear I felt as I started to allow myself to lean into my grief rather than cover it with happy pretense was palpable. I wasn't in control; I couldn't just smile and pretend I was fine. I imagine you might have a sense of that anxious, out-of-control feeling as well.

It makes me think of my buddy Tom. He and his wife visited local prisons weekly for decades. I wasn't sure that sort of thing was for me. Underneath that, I was scared. I was scared of what I did not know. I didn't think I'd have anything to offer the inmates. I felt out of my league pastorally. But after months of his boisterous invitations to join him, Tom finally wore me down. On the drive down to the prison, he could sense how tense and anxious I was feeling. I'll never forget him telling me to relax and be myself as we connected with the men behind bars.

"Just be you, Steve," Tom would say.

We went through the security checkpoint after presenting our identification and signing in. Grabbing my wallet, keys, and phone, I quickly caught back up with Tom. As we got closer to the cells, Tom started screaming: "LUJAH! LUJAH!"

I looked over at him like, *What are you doing, man?* It shocked me. He laughed and kept screaming the same word over and over. I finally said, "Tom, dude. What is that? Remember what you told me? Just be you; be cool."

He kept eye contact with me and then shouted, "LUJAH!" as loud as humanly possible with the biggest smile on his face.

"Carter, listen. LUJAH is my call sign. Every time I enter a prison, I scream it over and over. It's short for *hallelujah*—these men know it. When they come into this space, they feel alone and forgotten. Many of their families stop coming to see them, and I want them to know I will never stop coming after them. These men must know there is hope, even in a dark place like this! So if it's OK with you, Carter, I'm going to keep screaming, 'LUJAH!'"

As he screamed again, I heard a chorus of "LUJAH" coming back at us. The men knew, just like he said they would. Tom, this sixty-something-year-old man in a brown leather jacket and a mustache that would make Tom Selleck jealous, was here for them.

And he'd keep coming.

Lifting up a LUJAH!

No matter what.

I texted Tom recently. He's been sick, and it's not looking good. The circumstances are dire as the disease continues to take ground against his body. But within the first ten words he sent back to me, he reminded me of his call sign, his favorite word, and a motto that wasn't just for the incarcerated but now for him.

When you go from found and lost to found again, how can you not lift up a LUJAH?

The last verse of Psalms says, "Let everything that has breath praise the LORD. Praise the LORD" (150:6). I'm reading that verse as I think of Tom, and I hear his loud voice booming in the back of my head. Hallelujah means "Praise the Lord."[3] When you think you know the way and come to find out you were lost, it presents a profound opportunity to celebrate because you know you are on your way to being found once again.

I was found. LUJAH!

I was lost. LUJAH!

I am found again. LUJAH!

Reflection Questions

1. Where in your GBR Journey have you applied meaning-making that wasn't helpful or true? In what ways can you take some time to look back and change your perspective?

2. Much like the pilgrimage Steve took to Portugal, the process of grief is a pilgrimage, a sacred journey. Imagine you are on the trail now. What are some things you notice when you quiet your soul and listen to what it may be teaching you as you navigate your way?

PART 3

RECEIVE

Welcome to *Sunday*.

My friends, we've come to the third part of our GBR Journey, which I've affectionately dubbed *Receive*. After we've learned to sit in our grief and as we breathe, we are finally ready to receive the invitations that change extends to us. We have been honest about our pain, made room for it to air out and heal, and allowed for the possibility of hope and renewal. We've decided which parts of the past we can part with and which are too precious to leave behind. Our hard work has opened space for something new. Something that may even surprise us.

At this point, the trail incline tends to intensify and often we must find an inner strength to continue reaching for hope.

We have been climbing for so long. Take a moment to look back at the land you've crossed. Reminisce every challenge, celebrate all the ground you've taken, and prepare for what's ahead. What is next for you? Perhaps it's the surprise of what tomorrow might bring. Take a deep breath, open your palms, and prepare to *Receive*.

THE GRIEF JOURNEY

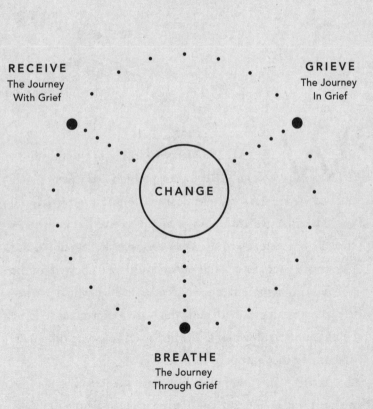

RECEIVE
The Journey
With Grief

GRIEVE
The Journey
In Grief

CHANGE

BREATHE
The Journey
Through Grief

CHAPTER 12

BREAKING BREAD

Who Are You Bound To?

There was a moment in a postgame press conference when the former Arizona Cardinals head football coach was asked about the Chicago Bears. In my humble opinion, he gave one of the greatest responses when he said, "They are who we thought they were, and we let 'em off the hook!"[1]

It's a quote my wife and I have often repeated since the fallout at Willow: "They are who we thought they were!" Yet part of us winces every time. Because the truth is, for a long time, we really thought they were different. We thought they were good. We thought they were honest. We thought they were brave. Each time we saw a new headline, someone sent us a clip, or we learned something new about the leadership choices being made we'd think, *They are who we thought they were*. We just wanted them to be better.

Knowing who an enemy is is one thing, because then their behavior isn't shocking. You kind of see it coming. The bar is low, so no one is surprised when they are crummy. But it's an entirely more painful feeling when you think you know someone and then find out they were fooling you the whole time.

That's the cognitive dissonance that comes with a betrayal of the personal kind, right?

During the reign of King David, there was a man the rabbis said had wisdom that bordered on that of the angels (2 Samuel 16:23). His name was Ahithophel, which in Hebrew meant "brother of ruin and folly." In every battle King David fought, he sought the advice of Ahithophel. They were close. They ate many meals together, and they built Jerusalem and Israel to be the superpower of the day.

One of David's sons, Absalom, spent time outside the city gates and heard the struggles of people from the various tribes. He slowly began to win the hearts of the people. They started to believe Absalom would have their back if he were king. Crowds began following him, demanding that Absalom become king rather than David. In a surprising turn of events, Ahithophel decided to side with Absalom to help him stage a coup on David's empire. When David realized what was happening, he cried out in various psalms, including:

If an enemy were insulting me,

I could endure it;

if a foe were rising against me,

I could hide.

But it is you, a man like myself,

my companion, my close friend,

with whom I once enjoyed sweet fellowship

at the house of God,

as we walked about

among the worshipers. (Psalm 55:12–14)

It's like David was saying, "Anyone but you, Ahithophel! I can handle anyone else but you. How could you?"

Even my close friend,

someone I trusted,

one who shared my bread,

has turned against me. (Psalm 41:9)

The "one who shared my bread" had David twisted inside. Bread was a staple at every meal. It provided sustenance, yes, but it also represented more. It served as a prop connecting people together around the table. To break bread with another was symbolic. The message was that if you broke off a piece of bread and handed it to someone and they ate it, they acknowledged that you were bound to each other.

Perhaps this is why Jesus modeled the power of sharing meals with those who didn't align with his values. Time and again, we see Jesus sharing bread with tax collectors, prostitutes, and other people deemed socially vile. If bread was on the table, there was a chance for reconciliation, peace, and a path of unity, if not friendship. Bread represents possibility. You might have shown up at that table as enemies, but by the time you finished your meal, you could leave bound to one another.

In John 13, we witness a moment when Jesus washes the disciples' feet. Context is helpful here because washing the feet of others wasn't something people with a rabbi status did. This messy chore was considered beneath them. And if you stop and think about it for a minute, it is not hard to understand why. I mean, the people of Jesus' day wore open shoes that exposed their feet to all kinds of disgusting things. We're not just talking dirt here, friends. Animal waste, urine, and filth would have been tracked on a person's feet. To sit and wash them was a disgusting and humiliating job.

I was telling my son about this as I was working on this chapter, and he promptly showed me a meme that said, on average, we lose half a pint of sweat from our feet each day. I mean, that is a very gross fact to know. *You're welcome!* We can add sweat to the list of gross things Jesus voluntarily touched on that day. Jesus was making a point in doing this: to show the disciples that his kingdom is one of service and flipping expectations on their heads. His kingdom centers on how low you can go and how you can lift others up. This lifestyle embodies suffering and sacrifice, and it believes repentance, truth telling, and reconciliation are always possible.

The disciples were uncomfortable having Jesus serve them in this way. As they began to understand what he was teaching, they slowly relaxed and embraced the tangible lesson he offered them. However, one of the disciples was growing increasingly frustrated with the type of revolution Jesus was offering. He expected the Messiah to come into the world, announcing war on the Roman Empire, rallying the troops, and leading a raid of bloodshed and vengeance.

As Jesus stood and dried his hands after washing the disciples' feet, he quoted David's psalm: "He who shared my bread has turned against me" (John 13:18).

The disciples were confused. Hadn't they all just submitted to Jesus' teaching about humility and a different kind of kingdom? Weren't they all there, gathered with him, supporting him and vowing to go with him to the end? Finally, one asked, "Lord, who is it?" (v. 25).

Jesus answered, "It is the one to whom I will give this piece of bread when I have dipped it in the dish" (v. 26).

The room, I have to imagine, was silent. Jesus broke a piece of bread, dipped it in a dish, and handed it to Judas. As we consider the symbolism of bread, we recognize this is, in some ways, an invitation that Jesus was extending to Judas. If he accepted the bread from Jesus and ate it, then Judas would be declaring that he was bound to his rabbi.

The passage says, "As soon as Judas had taken the bread, he went out" (v. 30).

Judas took the bread, but apparently he did not eat it. He left the table.

I can't even imagine what it would have been like at that moment to have been one of the disciples looking on, watching the scene unfold. Were they surprised? Or maybe they'd heard rumblings of dissatisfaction from Judas before. Did anyone go out after him? Did they have a million questions for Jesus after Judas left?

A Jesuit priest once said, "We never take Eucharist; we only receive it. *Taking* is what the man and woman did in the garden. It's something many of us do in our everyday lives, we take and climb and strive to advance; but when it comes to Christ's bread, grace, and invitation, all we can ever do is simply receive and eat."[2]

When Judas took the bread but did not eat it, it was as if he was saying, "Jesus, I'm not bound to you, your ways, or your kingdom anymore."

Jesus taught that every moment is brimming with redemptive potential, so even if he had a sense that Judas was turning against him, he still gave Judas the chance to receive and eat, to change his mind and stay the course with Jesus rather than follow through with his plan to betray him.

Jesus was saying, "Judas, you are not Ahithophel. It doesn't have to end like this."

The Scriptures tell us that after Ahithophel's plan was thwarted, King David regained power, and Ahithophel bought a plot of land and died by suicide (2 Samuel 17:23). Judas made a similar choice (Matthew 27:5).

When you desire connection, honesty, and reconciliation, and the other person chooses to reject your invitation, that hurts. It also hurts to watch someone you care about believe the lies that there is no hope and that when the shame of their decisions outweighs their belief in redemption, the only way out is to leave this world. That is an ache like no other. I believe Jesus wept when Judas took his life, and I also believe that, even at that moment, he wished for Judas to experience peace.

Often, when Communion is offered in a church service, it is presented as an opportunity to slow down, reflect on the sacrifice Jesus made on the cross, and give thanks for his ultimate act of selfless love. It is a practice that allows for many beautiful moments to be experienced. However, when we limit the experience to that expectation only, I believe we are missing out on a huge piece of the story. By receiving the bread and the cup, we are choosing to be bound to Jesus. We are, essentially, sitting at his table and allowing him to tear off a piece of bread and hand it to us; and, by eating it, we are saying yes to his kingdom ways.

I think for most of us, it's fairly easy to share meals with one another. It's not hard to align with others and find peace, even when we don't all have the same lifestyle or belief system. Most of the time, we can find enough common ground to come together and have peace. However, what about those who have wronged you, hurt your ego, gone behind your back, or betrayed you? Even when Jesus knew Judas would most likely betray him, he still offered him a chance to be bound again.

Now, I want to make an important note here. Pastors and

others have used this story for decades to force people back into dangerous and abusive situations under the language of reconciliation. It's important I make it abundantly clear that I am not suggesting anyone enter or remain in a relationship that causes harm or abuse. I am also not saying we should force ourselves into relationships with people we don't want to be with. When someone in authority attempts to force forgiveness and reconciliation onto a victim, it is malpractice and should not be tolerated. It also goes completely against what Jesus was showing us at that moment. Jesus didn't call on the other disciples to arm-wrestle Judas back to the table so he could force-feed him the bread. No. Jesus simply invited him, offered the choice, and allowed him to choose. Maintaining consent and free will is vital for our well-being and the well-being of any relationship.

I've come to realize that I'm responsible only for my heart, my body, my healing, and how I'm inviting God's love, grace, and truth into my everyday life. In each relationship, I have a choice to make, every single day. Will I offer a place at my table? Will I tear off bread and hand it to others in my life? Will I choose to accept the bread that is handed to me?

I think of Bill and the others who enabled him and kept his secrets. I think of the story I was told about my biological father and the truth that was kept from me. What role does bread play in those relationships? I may never know the answers or have the chance to find out. The real question is, Am I doing my work now to heal so that if one of them presents me with a genuine invitation of peace, I can make that decision from a whole and healthy place rather than a reactionary and volatile one?

I also believe it's important to clarify that reconciliation isn't always the goal. Reconciliation also isn't the only mark of healing or repair. Some relationships have ended, and that is just a fact. There is no need to resuscitate them. It helps to view reconciliation more as a peacemaking ritual for our inner selves rather than an outer commitment to renewing a relationship. We forgive on our own, and if possible, we reconcile with others. The goal is peace, not necessarily a relationship.

A key part of the reconciliation process is the importance of timing. Both parties involved need to be doing their work to heal and own their failings. For reconciliation to have a chance, repentance and truth telling must be involved. Betrayal trauma impacts us in many ways. It manipulates our trust and leaves us holding the bag of their fallout.

One practice I utilized that helped me work through the pain of this process involved writing out a dialogue, almost like a screenplay. I imagined what I would need to hear from someone who had harmed me. I wrote these words:

> Steve, I'm sorry for _____. I recognize that my actions hurt you. My goal wasn't to hurt you, but I know I did. Here is the work I've been doing to uncover why I did what I did. I've discovered _____ about myself. I don't have any excuses, but I want you to see how my unprocessed grief, trauma, and inability to do the hard

internal work have negatively impacted you, your heart, and your life. Here is what I plan to do to make amends and try my best to make it right: _____. Once I do this, I'd love to ask for your forgiveness.

Now, no bone in my body expects them to do this or ever say a version of these words to me. I get it. In their minds, I am in the past. However, in my mind, I want to find ways to be like Jesus. I want to keep the possibility of breaking bread with them in my heart, even if I never get to practice it with them in real life. My friend Tommy taught me that this type of thinking and living is what he refers to as "a context for a deeper relationship with Christ." It's an invitation to slow down and really engage with how Christ lived. It's a way to listen and learn from your Rabbi.

I can't shake the question, "How did Jesus keep his heart open?" How did he know all he did about the potential betrayal and still hand the bread to Judas? I would have been livid and made it known. I think of some specific moments before we left Willow when people betrayed me and said cruel things about me, sometimes behind my back and sometimes to my face. Even as I remember those moments, my body feels tense and my heart hurts. How did Jesus avoid resentment and retribution? Jesus offers us a path that leads not only to the exterior, global peace but also to a personal, inner peace. Instead of keeping angst and rage inside, replaying old wounds like game tapes, rewinding every memory and letting them continue to roil us up, we can choose to let them go.

When we do this, we learn to be more like Jesus, remaining grounded, centered, and open to the possibilities of peace that comes with a softened heart. Jesus lived every moment of his life with a deep belief that redemption is always possible.

Slowly but surely, Jesus is still kindly showing me a better way as he takes up more residence in my heart. I'm beginning to trust him even with this, and I'm starting to understand what it means to be bound to him even in this painful part as I acknowledge how betrayal has harmed me.

Reflection Questions

1. Take time to consider the things you are bound to. Are they serving you as you work toward healing? Is there anything you need to let go of or add?

2. Think of something that is a source of pain in your GBR Journey. This could be a person, a feeling, an experience, a memory, and so on. What role does bread have in that relationship?

CHAPTER 13

MIRACLES

What If Something Good Might Happen?

W hat does it take to make a miracle happen? And while we're at it, what is a miracle?

In the years I've spent connecting with people worldwide, I believe that forgiveness, honoring the truth, repentance, and humility are essential for reconciliation. And what, dear reader, is a miracle if not the act of reconciliation?

I believe in miracles.

I didn't always.

But I do now.

I was five when Joel adopted me. In one afternoon, I went

from Stephen Charles Born to Stephen Ryan Carter. My "new dad," as I commonly referred to him early on, was good to me. My memories of him, when I was little, are sweet and positive. He was patient and loved to play. We'd spend a lot of time outdoors because he loved nature. We'd spend hours playing with my Matchbox cars. He'd get down on the carpet beside me and tell me the names of each miniature automobile I'd hold up. I thought he was the coolest guy in the world and knew I was the luckiest kid to get to call him my dad. I'm sure subconscious parts of me felt insecure and needy for a father's love, but I consistently felt safe and secure with him as far as I can remember.

But as I got older, I began to see another side of him. He had unresolved anger that often spilled over into our relationship. He would blow up in a stream of rage and foul language at the drop of a hat. Some mornings, he'd yell if I used the wrong spoon with my cereal. Other mornings, he wouldn't say a word about it. Sometimes I would get verbally torn to pieces because I bit a tortilla chip too loudly. Once, he told me he didn't think I loved him because I'd loaded the dishwasher "wrong." I never knew what would set him off, which created a deep sense of anxiety for me as a teenager. I learned to read my dad's body language, looking for clues that would tell me if he was safe or dangerous by the tilt of his head or the set of his jaw. The emotional and verbal abuse was severe if I misread his body language.

On the days I would get it wrong, he'd cuss me out and tell me I was stupid, lazy, bad, selfish, and so on. It didn't seem to matter whether I spoke up, cried, or stood silently. Now I can see that he was never really yelling at me. He was angry with someone I couldn't see. Whether it was someone he wasn't reconciled with or a part of himself or someone in his past who'd hurt him, I'll never know. But I bore the brunt of his rage, and on those days, I'd find a reason to leave our house. I'd go to a friend's house or for a walk, but most often, I'd grab my basketball and head to the nearby park to shoot hoops until the sun went down. Basketball became my escape. It was my sanctuary to hide from the chaos at home.

For the most part, our relationship was stable, but there were still moments, even when I graduated and started college, that he would use his words and anger to rip me to shreds. I assumed he was right. There must be something wrong with me. I would try so hard to be perfect, to live up to his expectations for me, to be somehow able to read his mind. It was an impossible task, I know. But try telling that to a young man who desperately wants his father's love and acceptance. I would have done anything for him.

We were not religious, and the only reason I ended up in Christian schools was that my parents were convinced these private schools were better than the public options available. I'd always had a sense of right and wrong and a strong conviction to improve the world. I loved being around people and hearing their stories. It was only natural to make it official and become a Christian, which I did during seventh grade. Shortly after, I was baptized in the baptismal of my childhood church sanctuary.

I found an incredible and vibrant faith in the story of Jesus. I wanted my life to have purpose and kindness like his life did. I wanted my life to mean something. I wanted to matter, and back in the early 1990s, the overall message streaming from youth groups in America was that we all had a special calling, a divine purpose, and it was our task to find it and make a career of it. Back then, I had no idea what I wanted to do with my life, but I knew one thing for sure: I wanted it to be as much like Jesus as possible.

My parents' faith developed only after I left for college. On my nineteenth birthday, I was able to baptize my dad, a day I remember fondly. I was excited about the chance to share in this faith together. I hoped this would help us grow a strong and loving bond. In some small ways, over the years, I saw the beginnings of a transformation in him. Little by little, it seemed like the grace of Christ was taking up residency in his life, perhaps helping him heal some of his own emotional wounds.

But deciding to live a life of faith doesn't change who you are, and old coping skills die hard. There were still many moments of cruelty and efforts to control me and others in his life by verbally and emotionally abusive means. I still never knew what might set him off.

Over the next decade, a handful of moments sent me spiraling back to that eight-year-old little boy I used to be, hiding and running from my dad lashing out. The problem was, I wasn't eight anymore. I was a grown man, yet my dad's anger still held a terrifying power over me. I was still aching for his approval after all those years. Now that I was older, it was easier to identify the moments when he was abusive. I had started therapy for the first time, and as I realized parts of my relationship with my dad were dangerous and even toxic, I started to distance myself from him.

Shortly after I turned thirty-two, my dad sent me a letter that destroyed me. I can still remember how it felt the moment I opened it. I stared at each line, blinking back tears and stunned, barely breathing. My eyes scanned the words, registering familiar blows: "selfish . . . coward . . . hate . . . failure . . . disappointment." I couldn't breathe. How could these be the words of a father? Yet I quickly found myself spiraling down a familiar shame message: *Maybe I am all these things he says about me. Maybe he's right. I am worthless. No one could ever love me.*

Stop! Internally, some strength greater than me rumbled and stood up to the bullying of my inner voice of shame. *Stop! You are not worthless. You are loved. What is really happening here isn't about you, and you know that.* Perhaps I did know that somewhere deep inside, but it felt impossible to believe then.

I knew I had a choice to make at that moment: I could fall back into the old pattern with my dad and let him verbally abuse me whenever he wanted to, or I could decide I wanted something different and draw a boundary. I knew the answer but instantly felt the grief of loss. I knew it would be risky to stand up to him. His letter was a devastating blow to my heart and our relationship. I struggled to have any semblance of hope that it could be recovered.

For eighteen months, Joel and I didn't speak. And then, one morning while I was on a work trip in Charleston, South Carolina, I got a Facebook notification that someone had sent me a new message.

It was my dad.

I could feel the cortisol rushing into my body. We hadn't communicated in over a year and a half. Would this message be like the last letter he sent me? Was I ready to find out? I took a deep breath and clicked on the message: "Hi, Steve. I am sorry about the condition of our relationship, and I am sorry for what I have done to get us here. I am ashamed I have behaved badly. If a day comes when we could meet for coffee as two guys who want to be more like Jesus, I will enjoy that."

I sighed, feeling my arms and legs tingle as his words washed over me. I could barely process what I'd read. It was the first glimmer of hope, the beginning of repentance, humility, and honoring what actually had happened. I wrote him back, and we agreed to meet in person.

A few weeks later, I stood shaking in the parking lot of a little mom-and-pop hot dog stand halfway between Chicago and Grand Rapids. I couldn't believe I was about to see my dad again after so much time and pain had passed between us. I was nervous and scared, but I was also curious. And despite years of evidence to the contrary, I was also hopeful for a real change.

I took a deep breath and steadied myself, then I opened the door. A tiny bell dinged, alerting the patrons to my arrival. There, sitting at a table in the back, was my dad. I knew it was him even before he turned around. The set of his shoulders was softer, somehow. His face was a little gentler. His eyes seemed older. Without saying it, we both understood the stakes.

During the next hour and a half, Joel told me about his grief over our relationship and how he wished it had been different. He told me he had gone through a significant transformation. He asked for a chance for us to get to know each other again. He also allowed me to consent without pressure, knowing that if I didn't want to, he would have to accept that. Before we left, we decided to meet at the same spot again the following month.

And slowly, ever so gently, something good began to happen.

Each month, a profoundly different version of my dad came into view. Whenever he opened his mouth, he'd say something I was not expecting. His cadence was different. There was humility in his phrasing. There was grace in the way he encouraged me. I could feel his love in the tone. I let down my guard and let this new dad back into my heart.

Those monthly hot dog stand visits led to calls during the week, regular connection, and keeping up with what was happening in each other's lives like old friends do. We started getting together with the family, and my kids finally got to know their grandfather and his sweet wife, Judy. My kids adored him and affectionately called him "Blue Papa" (for the University of Michigan). We were finding the good.

The funny thing is, the good in our relationship didn't

start at that hot dog stand, and it didn't start with the Facebook message from my dad. In truth, the good started the day I drew a line and said no more. It started when I read his letter and decided I wanted something different. I did not want the kind of relationship I had *then* with my dad; I wanted more. I wanted to love and be loved. I wanted to respect and be respected. I wanted a relationship that could hold me and celebrate me and support me, and I wanted to be able to offer those things back to him as well. I took a chance, partly out of desperation but also out of a pure and ridiculous hope.

The distance we experienced during those eighteen months actually served a greater good. It was like a controlled burn that removes dangerous and pervasive growth so a healthier new life can thrive. The distance allowed both of us to look inward. It caused me to see how my wounds had taken root and affected my daily life not only in my relationship with my dad but also in how I partnered with Sarah, parented my kids, and interacted at work. The break also allowed me to start untangling the roots and discovering what was in my garden. Growing right beside my fear were other weeds: resentment, bitterness, control, insecurity. Below the surface, my wounds were tangling up my ability to receive love, to actually love myself and others well. I wanted to cultivate a healthy and robust love, and as I went to therapy and examined my life, I started to do just that.

In the same way, my dad had been undergoing a similar transformation, digging into why he was angry and doing the brave work of facing his inner wounds. He had to sit with the memories of the pain he had caused my younger self and grieve that. He had to work hard to develop new coping skills and to love those he loved. Even while we were apart, Joel and I were doing parallel work. We were both fighting for the chance to grow better, not bitter. We both refused to give up on ourselves and on the hope that one day, we might have the chance to heal what had been broken and start fresh.

In your own life, has there been a time when you've had a similar experience? Maybe a relationship where you wonder if reconciliation is even possible? You can learn to not give up, but rather to see this season as one in which you're living in the waiting well by allowing the Spirit to go to work on your heart. For many years I easily could write someone off and quite honestly waste the wait by believing that change wasn't possible. But that mindset also believes that our perspective can't change either. The surrendered life does the harder work to stay wide open to a miracle.

All of it culminated in that first conversation when we chose to meet at that old roadside spot, sitting across from each other and eager for a chance to begin again: me as new Steve, and Joel as new Dad.

To this day, it was one of the holiest conversations I've ever experienced.

It was nothing short of a miracle.

Reflection Questions

1. Do you believe in miracles? Why or why not?
2. If you could experience one miracle, what would it be and why?
3. Does someone come to mind as you read this chapter? Take time to consider why and what role you could play to bring healing into the relationship.

CHAPTER 14

YELLOW BUG

So You're Saying There's a Chance?

Early in my work in ministry, I was employed by a church in Michigan. Sarah and I bought a little house in Grand Rapids, one town from where my dad, Joel, lived. One day while driving downtown on my way to a meeting, I passed by an old yellow Volkswagen Bug and thought of my dad. Whenever I see them, he comes to mind because he had one when he was younger and often recounted stories about his adventures over the years. After parking, I took my phone from my pocket and dialed his number. It rang and went to voicemail.

"Hey, Dad. Just walking and saw a yellow Bug. Made me think of you. Love you."

I'll never forget where I was standing when he called back. He told me he hadn't felt well for a while and was pretty sure he had mono. He was very fatigued and lacked the usual energy to start the day. The doctors took some blood and sent it off to the lab. The next day my dad got a call informing him that his white blood cell count was six times greater than it was supposed to be. They rushed him to the hospital. Within a few days, the doctors diagnosed him with acute myelogenous leukemia. This form of cancer is aggressive and relentless, especially for someone my dad's age.

For the next four months, my dad stayed at a phenomenal oncology hospital in downtown Grand Rapids while the expert doctors gave him rounds of chemotherapy treatments. We would visit nearly every day, taking turns after work or during lunch breaks to check in with him. As anyone who has gone through chemo can attest, it takes a significant toll on the body. My dad was weak, but his hope remained high.

At the end of my dad's treatment, his doctors informed us that he had gone into remission. I'm sure you could hear our cheers for several blocks as we celebrated with relief such happy news. We were told the goal was for him to make it five years cancer-free. If he could do that, then he would be in the clear. There was so much hope in that hospital room.

A few weeks later, we were at my dad's house celebrating that he was home and in remission when he received a phone call. I remember standing beside him in his kitchen.

He was making his world-famous chicken burritos, teaching me his perfect recipe. I'd had a flashback to when I was little, and he was having a good day, music blaring on the radio, a Michigan football game on the TV, and the heavenly scent of those burritos wafting from my childhood kitchen. His phone rang again, jolting me back to the present. He handed me his spatula and stepped out of the room. I knew it was terrible even before he came back in. I was shaking as he hung up and struggled to make eye contact with me.

"Dad? What is it?" I gently asked.

"That was, uh . . . that was my doctor, bud. When I went back yesterday for my routine blood work tests, they discovered that the cancer came back . . ." His voice trailed.

I was frozen. I literally couldn't move. Sarah, who had been in the other room, came running and grabbed us both by the shoulders, pulling us into a group huddle in his kitchen. It was impossible to tell whose tears were whose, all of us too overcome to speak, letting our shock and grief spill out all over the linoleum floor.

When the goal is five years, and you don't even make it five weeks before having a relapse, it's not a good sign. Over the next few days, his doctors told us the only chance for survival was for my dad to have a bone marrow transplant from a suitable match. Since I was adopted, I wasn't a viable option. The doctors searched the international donor bank, and out of ten million registrants (six million within the US and four million outside the US), only one person was a complete match.

When the doctor told my dad that he had a one in ten million chance of survival, he quickly quoted *Dumb and Dumber* and said, "So you're saying there's a chance." Even the doctor cracked a laugh at that. Joel always had a way of changing the mood of a room, and when he used it for good, it was an incredible feeling. And we desperately needed that moment of levity because we all knew the stakes were so high.

The donor who was a perfect match and my dad's only hope of survival was a woman in her thirties who lived in the United Kingdom. The process is kept private and anonymous to help protect the privacy of both parties, so we simply had to wait while the medical team contacted her and asked if she would be willing to donate. It's a painful experience, extracting bone marrow from the donor's hip with a massive needle. There was a good chance that she would not choose to go through that for a stranger she didn't know halfway across the globe. We had to brace ourselves for the possibility of disappointment.

While we waited, my dad was transferred to Ann Arbor, to the University of Michigan Hospital, to prepare him in case the transplant was a go. He needed around-the-clock care and had to be very careful to avoid germs, as his immune system was already weak and would be further compromised during recovery if the bone marrow was donated. Ann Arbor was farther away for us and prevented us from going to visit every day, but we'd make it down at least once a week. The gap between visits made his decline more obvious. Each time we'd see him, he would be smaller and paler. He was losing hope and beginning to shut down emotionally.

During that dark time, Sarah and I found out we were going to be parents. We were beyond thrilled and wanted to find a way to share our happy news with my dad while still respecting the hard and scary place he was at in life. We arranged for Sarah to have an ultrasound early so that we could bring the sonogram with us to the hospital when we visited my dad. We put it in an envelope and took it with us as we headed down to Ann Arbor.

When we walked into his hospital room, it was dimly lit, and the beeping sounds of his monitor were steady. My dad had been sleeping, and he slowly opened his eyes and turned his head to look our way. I couldn't believe how quickly he was declining now. Sarah placed the envelope in his shaky hands. I crouched beside his bed, watching as he slowly opened the paper and pulled out the black-and-white image.

He looked at the picture, looked at Sarah, looked back at the picture, and exclaimed, "I'm gonna be a grandpa?"

With tears in our eyes, we nodded.

He began laughing. "I'm gonna be a *grandpa*! Now I gotta get well! And I will!"

Before we ever met Emerson, he was the surprising gift that inspired my dad to keep going.

The following day, the donor kindly agreed to provide her bone marrow to save my dad's life, and within forty-eight hours, my dad had a bone marrow transplant. People often ask me why I love the University of Michigan so much.

Maybe it's because when I was growing up, my dad and I would watch the Wolverines football team play on Saturdays in the fall. It was a way I could connect with my dad. No matter what was going on, we could always talk about Michigan football. And now, Dad's life was extended largely because of the University of Michigan's extraordinary doctors. That extra time allowed me to reconcile with my dad, work through the past, and become the best of friends in the remaining years of his life.

We knew the new bone marrow had to attach to my dad. Sometimes it does not, which is referred to as graft-versus-host disease: the transplanted marrow sees the host body as a disease and begins attacking it. Doctors want a little bit of this because it shows that the marrow and body connect, but too much can be deadly. My dad's body changed during this time. He lost all his teeth, his skin became very thin, and the most minor cut caused significant bleeding. His oxygen levels were challenging, he could lose breath quickly, and he often had an oxygen tank on him. His immune system was also compromised, so we had to wear masks and be conscientious about keeping him safe from germs.

But *he was alive*. The transplant worked.

We were so grateful.

When Sarah delivered Emerson, my dad was in the waiting room, anxiously awaiting the moment he would meet the baby who'd given him a reason to fight for his life. From that day on, he carried in his wallet a small photograph taken in the hospital room after Emerson was born. In it, my dad is holding a tiny, swaddled baby, and my grandpa and I are standing on either side with our arms around my dad. Shortly after, Joel was interviewed by the *Grand Rapids Press*. When they asked him what having the bone marrow transplant meant to him, he said these words:

> It meant that my father didn't have to bury his other son. It meant that my son didn't lose his father in the prime of life. And it meant that this child would grow up to know me through a relationship and not just through pictures.[1]

We spent as much time together as we possibly could. When my work called me to Chicago, we relied on FaceTime for his daily fix of connection with Emerson. My toddler son would put the phone in his pocket and walk all over the house, narrating to my dad, who would laugh and laugh as he tried to make out what the little guy was saying. He loved having the time to connect with his grandson, no matter what they were doing together.

My dad fell in love with his nurse, an incredible woman named Judy. They later married in a plot twist that felt like a real-life Nicholas Sparks novel. She is one of the best humans who has ever lived. When they would come to Chicago to visit us, my dad always seemed to have energy. When I asked Judy about it, she told me that he would take extra steroids to relieve his pain to be present with us. She said he would sleep for days afterward, recovering from the cost of all that energy and output. He never regretted it. He wanted to soak up every second of life he could.

It was so healing watching him love my kids so well.

A little over four months after we moved to Arizona, Judy called me to say I needed to get to Grand Rapids quickly. Things weren't looking good for Dad. His graft-versus-host disease had progressed, and the toll it was taking on his body had turned his medical care from prevention to making him as comfortable as possible. I got off the phone, my hands shaking. None of this was a surprise. We knew this moment was coming. Every single day we got with him after his transplant was a bonus. A gift. We all knew that. And yet, I wasn't ready. I wanted more time.

I bought a ticket for the next flight to Grand Rapids, packed a bag, and headed to the airport. I barely reached my gate, sprinting and yelling to hold the doors as they were about to close them. I took my seat on the plane, sweating and panting, my eyes filled with tears. I'm sure I looked like a total mess. I *was* a total mess. I spent the entire flight willing the plane to go faster. I didn't want to miss my chance to say goodbye to my dad one last time.

I got to Grand Rapids, grabbed a rental car, and drove straight to the hospice hospital to see my dad. Right before entering his room, I stopped and took a deep breath. I knew what was on the other side of that door. I said a prayer and turned the handle.

The room was quiet except for the sound of the oxygen machine pumping air through his lungs and the heart monitor beeps that let me know I wasn't too late. I rushed to his bedside, buried my head in his chest, and took his hand, squeezing it so he would know I was there. He was silent but alert. He squeezed my hand back. He knew I was there.

I looked up and met Judy's eyes, both of us overcome with emotion. I was so thankful she was there in the room with me then. Her years as an oncology nurse were a blessing as she courageously stayed present and calm, allowing us to grieve and not fear the death that was unfolding. More of his family came and went. We told stories. We even laughed as we recalled some of his quips and memories over the years. It was all very cathartic. We cried, but honestly, it was not a tragic grief. It felt more like a peaceful grief, one full of gratitude.

He squeezed my hand again.

And that night, he passed peacefully in his sleep.

It's as if he knew we would all be OK, and he could go. He was tired and had fought for so long to stay with us. Just before he stopped talking, he had told me he was ready to see Jesus. I will always be grateful for that. Knowing he was ready to go helped me be prepared to let him go.

When I flew back home to Arizona, Sarah and the kids surrounded me in the driveway. We stood still for a long time, hugging, crying, and praying. Afterward, I took the dog for a walk. I needed to stretch my legs and get my bearings. The last few days had been a whirlwind of emotion, and I felt I needed time to process it with God.

As I was walking, I noticed a new family had moved into one of the townhomes. Coming up to their house, I gasped. Sitting right in front of the house was a 1968 yellow Volkswagen Bug, the same one my dad had in college. It hadn't been there before I left. I stopped walking and stared at it, taking in the magnitude of the moment. I swear, I could hear my dad's dry laugh echoing somewhere in the distance. *Hey, bud. Love you.*

Part of my work as a pastor is sitting with families as they grieve and helping them prepare for funerals, sometimes delivering the eulogy on their behalf. In grief counseling, I'd heard stories of moments like this one. Sometimes a feeling, song, or memory floats to the surface and feels weightier than an ordinary moment. Families have told me stories about visions, dreams, or something they experienced in creation shortly after a loved one died. Maybe you can relate, having experienced something similar after losing a loved one. My wife's family told me a story about hummingbirds when her grandma passed. Now every time they see one, it reminds them of her. On the day my dad passed, my wife saw a double rainbow, and to this day, whenever she sees a rainbow, it reminds her of Blue Papa.

And now I have a yellow Bug story.

Every morning, I see that yellow Bug. It's there when I wake before sunrise to walk the dog, and it's there when I get home from work. I often sit down on the curb right beside it. Sometimes I'm silent. Sometimes I talk about my day, and sometimes I pray. Whenever we drive by it, my daughter says, "Hi, Blue Papa!" To be clear, I don't think my dad has been reincarnated into a 1968 yellow Volkswagen Bug. But in the meaning-making, it has felt very kind of God to provide me with a way to feel connected to my dad even after his death. In an unlikely way, that yellow Bug is shifting something inside me.

As I'm trying to live more present to the moment and to remain open to the good and hard and everything in between, I'm practicing praying, "Oh Lord, surprise me today." I will take a deep breath and say, "Oh Lord," and let myself exhale, saying, "surprise me today." It's something I've come to do often throughout the day. I don't want to miss the thin places anymore. I want to be present in the holy moments that are so moving and sacred that all we can do is sit on a curb and soak them in. You're standing on holy ground.

On a chilly fall morning, as the sun is peeking over the mountains near our home, I again stand across from the yellow Bug. It is almost glowing as sunlight glints off its vintage metal mirrors. I sit down on the curb and talk to my dad:

Thank you, Dad, for doing the work and teaching me how to live well. Thank you for choosing to adopt me. You changed my life, and I wouldn't be who I am without you. Thank you for choosing to fight, try, and live another day so you could become the most incredible husband for Judy, dad for me, and grandpa for my kids. I love you. I miss you. Go Blue.

Reflection Questions

1. As you read this chapter, what came to mind in your own personal understanding of loss? How did it feel? What did it bring up for you? Write it down.

2. Steve shared about seeing yellow Bugs as a way to feel connected with his dad after he passed. Have you ever experienced something similar in your GBR Journey?

3. Do you have an old memory of a loved one who has passed away? Take a moment to sit with it and express gratitude for the gift of that relationship.

CHAPTER 15

HOMECOMING

Where Do You Want to Go?

We grieve many things: people we've lost, diagnoses, infidelity, missed opportunities, the ends of friendships, and pets that have passed on. We grieve our childhoods and aging parents. We grieve as we age, as well. Even if we embrace what is ahead, the past is irrevocably intertwined with grief. So I'm curious, have you ever grieved a place?

As I mentioned earlier in the book, my family and I left our home in a suburb outside Chicago about six months after the events at Willow in 2018. The move was incredibly hard, partly due to the nature of the exit. All the sadness and stress after leaving Willow made our move feel more like a desperate exile than a new and exciting endeavor. The truth is, we expected that home to be the home that housed all our kids' childhood memories. We had planted trees in the backyard as seedlings, expecting to watch them grow alongside Emerson and Mercy. We knew each creaky floorboard and had grown accustomed to the impossibly tiny bathrooms considered fashionable for some reason in the 1970s. It was, of course, less about the actual house and more about what it represented: a rootedness. A place to cultivate memories and love and connection. A safe harbor, a place our kids and both of us could count on. A home to return to on long weekends for laundry and home-cooked meals on those future college days. Leaving it cut deep.

Arizona proved to be exactly what we needed to begin healing from the trauma we had experienced in Illinois. It was a privilege that we could leave. I recognize that now, although it felt more like a punishment at the time. It felt wrong to be packing up our lives and saying goodbye to our friends, home, and the future we had expected. Watching our kids cry themselves to sleep, having to be present as they processed their anger and heartbreak, hurt like hell. I didn't have good answers for them. Most of the time, I didn't know how to answer their questions when they'd ask me why we had to move away. Why? The walls were closing around us, and we couldn't leave the house without having someone stop us to yell or cry, usually a combination of both.

I couldn't get enough work to support us in Chicago, and

Sarah couldn't walk through the grocery store without having a panic attack. We needed to get away. It was the only way we were going to find some semblance of normalcy and safety so we could begin to unpack our pain and trauma. But how do you explain that to your kids? You can't, really. At least not right away. So most nights we just sat beside them and let them cry, and we would cry too.

We started to get some space to process and grieve in Phoenix. I was traveling nonstop for work, taking every opportunity to speak at churches and conferences so we could pay our bills. After the pandemic hit, Sarah became a supplemental homeschool teacher as the kids started virtual school online. It was such a lonely time in our lives.

I learned during that time that loneliness isn't necessarily bad. In many ways, the loneliness was necessary. We had to empty ourselves to learn the sound of our own voice again. We had to remove the voices of others—the judgment and sorrow and anger and expectation—all of it had to go in order for us to begin healing.

An unexpected thing began to happen as our world got smaller and quieter. We turned toward each other. We learned how to really listen to ourselves and each other. We discovered what we wanted for our futures, named some new hopes, and shared what we were learning about how we were recovering from the trauma of Willow.

Our goal as parents has always been to help our kids recognize their agency. We want them to grow up knowing they can name and express their desires. Growing up, I struggled to do this, often thinking that what my parents desired came first and foremost. It wasn't until my counselor suggested that I read *The Drama of the Gifted Child* by Alice Miller that I began to understand how disconnected I was from my desires and how connected I was to fulfilling my parents' wishes.[1]

The summer before Emerson started eighth grade, Sarah and I began to talk about what we wanted his high school experience to be like. Emerson has always been an old soul, gravitating to deeper conversations and endlessly curious about the world around him. His wisdom has always exceeded his age, and after going through the pain of leaving Willow and moving away from his childhood friends, he went through a dark time. He wasn't interested in making new friends, which I understood. He already had amazing friends. They just lived over two thousand miles away now. Why should he go to the trouble of making new friends if there was a possibility they could be ripped away from him too?

When we moved away from Illinois, we pulled Emerson and Mercy out of their neighborhood elementary school halfway through the school year, moving just after Christmas. To this day, Mercy tells me she was sad she didn't get to say goodbye to her friends and teachers. They started their second semesters in a new school in Arizona, one full of kids who already had their friendship circles and weren't interested in adding any new ones.

Most nights, Emerson would go online and play video games with his friends in Chicago. Every Friday, they had a standing tradition to watch the same movie together, adjusting for the time changes and pushing Play simultaneously. Then they would jump on a FaceTime call and talk through the whole thing. Hearing these boys' countdown—"3, 2, 1, hit Play!"—was precious and painful.

As we began thinking about whether Arizona would be the place we put down roots and chose to stay for Emerson's high school years, I realized that I felt a deep connection with the Midwest. It's hard for me to explain fully, but when I'd walk into a space there, whether it was a church, a company boardroom, or a team's locker room—it just felt like home.

As I processed this with one of my mentors, he reminded me that the right place has the ability to empower us to be the fullest expression of who God makes us to be. We might consider a calling synonymous with a gifting, but that's not how the first church understood it. We can be called to a place, a city, a neighborhood, a state, or even a type of geography.

His insight reminded me of a time when I was in fifth grade and the social trend was to have themes. Well, maybe that was just a thing my friends and I did. We were quirky! But we chose things to represent us all the time. Which Ninja Turtle were you? Which type of dinosaur? What color is your color? I remember we all got together and chose the city, basketball team, and favorite players from that place that would represent us for life. It was a strong fifth-grade commitment, and we were serious about it.

Andy chose Portland and Clyde Drexler.

Ken chose Los Angeles and Magic Johnson.

Troy chose Detroit and Isiah Thomas.

Jeff chose Philadelphia and Charles Barkley.

Greg chose San Antonio and David Robinson.

Nick chose Boston and Larry Bird.

I chose Chicago and Michael Jordan.

We made a pact to buy an oversize puffy Starter jacket from our favorite NBA team (does anyone else remember those?). As we were growing up in Southern California, our crew dressed in shorts and oversize puffy jackets must have been quite a sight.

I had, in some unique ways, been a Midwest kid my whole life.

My friend Daniel Grothe wrote a book called *The Power of Place*, in which he unpacked how the early church mothers and fathers took a vow of stability.[2] I had the honor of endorsing it, and as I read through it, I was struck by how deeply his words spoke to me. He detailed how our culture today is more disconnected from a place than ever before. He recounted how early church leaders used to move to a place and buy a home and a cemetery plot. Their entire expectation was that they would live in the same place, focusing on the community and serving the city, for their entire lives. I remember reading this book on a plane and tearing up. I felt like my place was Chicagoland, but when we left Willow and moved away, I never imagined we could return. I appreciated Arizona, but it didn't feel like home.

Daniel's book was a key part of the conversation that Sarah and I were having in regard to where we wanted to put down roots for our kids' future school years. We had seen the impact moving midway through a school year had on them and wanted very much to land somewhere we could stay, regardless of what happened with a job. Never again did we want to have to move or change our lives because of someone else's scandal. As I wondered aloud where we should go for Emerson's high school years, Sarah suggested I ask him directly what he wanted.

Over pizza at our favorite spot, I asked him if he had thought about where he wanted to go to high school. Due to the nature of my work, we could go anywhere we wanted. Southern California, North Carolina, Portland, Hawaii, Europe, Colorado? I looked at him and asked, "Where would you want to go?"

Without missing a beat, he simply said, "I want to go home."

"Home?" I said.

"To our old neighborhood," he replied.

I shrugged and tried to seem neutral, not wanting to squash his dreams. Internally, I didn't see that as a possibility. We agreed to keep considering the question, paying attention to our desires and what came up around the idea over the following weeks.

When I shared our conversation with Sarah, she sat on the couch with her laptop open. "Hey, come look at this!" she said slyly.

I raised an eyebrow and sat beside her. She flipped her screen and showed me a house listing across the street from our closest friends back in Chicago.

I looked at her in shock. "You're in on this too? You want to move back?"

She shrugged. "What I want matters. Of course, it does. And at first blink, I wanted to be in Arizona near my extended family. I want to be able to go for walks and watch quail line my back fence. This is home for me. But what I really want is for our kids to be where they feel at home. And they both know Illinois is that for them. As parents, that's our work. We had to take them away from so much, for so long. Now is our chance to give them back some agency. To show them that when they tell us what they need, we hear them. This feels like a defining moment for us to take back our story as parents. At the end of the day, that's what I want the most. Our trauma doesn't get to write our story forever. Now we are taking it back."

Later that day, I called Daniel and shared with him what his book was stirring within us and what we saw next for our family. I asked him, "Does this even make sense?"

He responded by quoting a passage from Ezekiel: "I the LORD have rebuilt what was destroyed and have replanted what was desolate" (36:36). As he said those words, I was in tears. He was quoting the verse Sarah and I had chosen to be a guiding post for our relationship. Daniel didn't realize it, but Ezekiel 36:36 was the vision we'd set for our marriage and life's work. We had even chosen to be married on March 6 because of it.

Then Daniel said, "Remember Steve, it was Francis *of* Assisi, Teresa *of* Calcutta, Benedict *of* Nursia, Teresa *of* Avila,

Gregory *of* Nyssa . . . and you're Steve *of* Chicagoland. Accept it, brother, and join God in rebuilding the ruins!"

I called another wise mentor of mine, Dr. Paul Alexander. He's the president of my alma mater and a unicorn because he has degrees in organizational leadership, counseling, and biblical studies. He's one of my favorite people on the planet. When everything imploded at Willow, he and my preaching professor surprised me by flying out to spend time with me. It was a moving gesture, and having two wise men join me in my grief as I weighed what to do next was a blessing. I'll never forget, though, when Dr. Alexander told me not to leave Willow in one of our conversations. He never thoroughly explained why, so when we were considering this move back, I called him for advice as I often do.

He said, "You remember when I told you in 2018 not to leave Willow? I said that because my dad was a pastor, too, and he moved me when I was in elementary school. It messed with me for a while, but I'll never forget the gift my dad gave me when we moved back so that I could go to high school with my friends. It was one of the greatest gifts my dad ever gave me. You and Sarah are about to give this to your kids. They will always know you hear them and will do anything for them."

Later that month, Sarah and I made an offer on a home in our old neighborhood, and the summer before Emerson started his first year of high school, we moved twenty doors down from where we used to live. None of this would have been possible had we not embraced the healing work we each had to do before we could have returned to a place that had harbored so much pain. Had we tried to shortcut our way through grief, we would have crumbled at the first encounter with our past. We took four years and let ourselves feel it all. We told the truth, let it be messy, and refused to temper the reality of debris left in our trauma's aftermath. We never thought we'd move back. That was not our goal when we left.

However, in our case, going back was part of our story. There are still moments when PTSD hits. Some days, Sarah can't go to the grocery store because she feels triggered and afraid of running into certain people in the cereal aisle. I still get anxious when I see someone from Willow in the Starbucks line. *Will they confront me? Are they angry?* Our bodies remember all of it. Yet I know who I am after it all fell apart, and no one can take that away from me.

On a Friday evening just before sunset, Emerson joined his childhood friends at his first high school dance, for homecoming. They danced and laughed and had the best time. When I picked him up afterward, he was beaming. He felt home. He *was* home. And all felt right with the world as I blinked back tears at the miracle it is to be here.

To be able to come home again.

Reflection Questions

1. Have you ever had to move away from a place you loved? In what ways did that experience affect you?

2. Take a moment to check in with yourself. Place your hand over your heart. Take deep breaths. What does it feel like to be present to the place you are in right now?

CHAPTER 16

FINISH LINE

What Race Are You Running?

A friend of mine was recently telling me about the training she was undergoing in preparation for the Chicago Marathon. It sounded brutal; from the early morning wake-ups to the multi-mile training runs, I was equal parts impressed with her tenacity and thankful that I was *not* running the Chicago Marathon. It did remind me of the last time I'd run a 5K, which was all the way back when I was in college, and my friend Jeff asked me to run a race with him. When I asked him why we'd ever want to do that, he told me his family had been running the same race for years. Apparently, if you run the race, you get to go out for a steak dinner afterward—and for two poor college kids, that sounded like a pretty good deal.

"Run for a steak? I'll do that!" I exclaimed.

On the morning of the race, I walked toward the starting line and found my friend and his family. I had some time before the start and figured a quick run to the restroom would be smart. As I returned from the porta potty, a considerably large group of runners had gathered toward the starting line.

A minute later, the emcee blared, "All right, runners! Five. Four. Three. Two. One. Goooo!"

I joined the group and took off. I couldn't find my friend or his family members, but I figured I'd catch up with them sometime during the race. As I ran, I couldn't help but notice it was taking a while. I was getting winded when a guy in his seventies passed me. I was too exhausted to be embarrassed, and honestly, I was impressed with his stamina!

I pushed to catch up with him and casually asked, "Hey, man. Whew! It feels like we've been running for a while now. How far do we still have to go?"

The man looked at his watch and replied, "We just hit the five-mile mark. Eight point one to go!"

I almost tripped. *Five miles? Eight more to go?* He must have noticed my face because he raised his eyebrow and gave me an inquisitive stare. I looked at him and shouted, "I thought this was the 5K!"

He laughed and said, "You're running the wrong race, dude!"

I slowed down and had a choice to make. I could stop

running, find my friend, and make him buy me that steak dinner *and* dessert for my trouble, or I could finish this half-marathon race. Part of me wasn't sure if I could finish it, and that part convinced me I had to at least try. My pride was on the line, although I'm pretty sure that ship sailed the moment the grandpa zoomed by me.

When I finally saw the finish line, I could make out my buddy's silhouette. He looked refreshed and excited, cheering me on. I wanted to scream. None of this was his fault, but I discovered during this half-marathon that bitterness was an excellent motivator.

I crossed the finish line, sweat dripping from my forehead and my whole body shaking.

"Dude, you ran the wrong race!" my friend laughed as he ran to me.

"No kidding. I can't feel my legs," I uttered, panting and bending over.

A woman who had run with me came up and unzipped her neon pink fanny pack, pulling out a smooshed peanut butter sandwich and handing it to me. "You don't look so good, kiddo. Eat this."

Having left my pride on the side of the road eight miles back, I opened my hand and let her place two triangle halves into my palm. They were noticeably warm, which should have made me cringe, but I was too carb-deprived to care. I shoved the whole thing in my mouth, maintaining direct eye contact with my friend. The horror on his face was the only reward I needed.

I skipped the steak dinner that night and was asleep by
7:00 p.m.

You're running the wrong race. The words jolted me out of
a lucid sleep. Had I dreamed them? Something about those
words hit deep. There was a weight to them that I sensed was
about more than a mistaken footrace.

I was at a crossroads in my life, trying to decide if I should
continue studying film or shift to pastoral work. I had always
planned to choose a career in the movie industry, but several
moments in that span of my life seemed to be redirecting me
toward a life of ministry. I'd tried to ignore it, but as I stopped
fighting and let myself really consider the possibilities, I knew
in my heart it was what I wanted to do. I changed my major
and pursued a preaching degree, jumping into a new sphere
and gaining network connections with churches and pastors.
I had never been so fulfilled and certain I was finally running
the race I was meant to.

I've spent more than twenty years serving the church as
a pastor. I've met incredible people of diverse backgrounds
across the globe, in Chile, Southern California, Nova Scotia,
Burundi, Palestine, Rwanda, and beyond. In each of those
places, I've walked alongside some of the most difficult and
painful parts of people's lives as they grieved loss and unexpected challenges. I have also celebrated beautiful wins and
successes. Through it all, I have learned so much, and I look
back with compassion at the younger versions of myself who
were trying earnestly to be the best I could be.

Someone recently asked me if I regretted becoming a

pastor after everything fell apart at Willow. I can under-stand their question. The church is wrought with pain and corruption, just like anywhere else. Pastors sin, just like everyone else. People on staff make decisions out of fear, just like everyone else. Community fails, friendships break down, and relationships are lost. This is part of the human experience, and following Jesus doesn't prevent us from it. There is no magic force field around the church that makes it any less likely to succumb to choosing fear over love. I realize my saying that might upset some people, but it is true. All you have to do is open social media or flip on the news to hear another story detailing allegations of miscon-duct, cover-up, and abuse against another church or pastor. Following a religion does not make us immune to the tempta-tion to manufacture our own salvation through sin. In fact, pretending to be invincible enables us to become another headline of moral failure.

During the crisis at Willow, the women who had been harmed by Bill had spoken up. They had not run away. They had stood up and done the courageous thing. There was a turning point when I knew I needed to speak up, too, but I feared the cost. I feared I had everything to lose if I did what I knew was right—and I hesitated.

Friend, let me tell you, when you get serious about over-coming a culture of fear that has kept everyone else shaking in their seats, people will try to shut you up. People close to you will try to bring you down. Why? Because, if they acknowl-edge your willingness to risk, then they will either have to stand with you or they will have to acknowledge their intention to resist.

At Willow, I discovered that years of efforts to speak up and penetrate a heavy blanket of fear were resisted with a fierce determination—all based on the thought that there was too much to lose. My own acts of courage, such as they were, came because I was inspired by the courage of others. The more I learned about the allegations and the processes that followed, the clearer it became that I was standing on the shoulders of others who had gone before me, advocating for authenticity, confession, clarity, and healing. There is a legacy that we weave for those who will come after us, and we are either cutting a path they will someday travel, or we are adding barricades that will inhibit their journey. Every choice we make lays a brick next to others, forming either a pathway or a wall, depending on our faithfulness to what God has asked of us.

Part of what I love about Jesus is that he lived his life in alignment with the practices of love. What we learn about him in the Scriptures paints a picture of kindness, humility, patience, honesty, integrity, and compassion. It's hard to argue with those qualities and the benefits of living in alignment with them, right? I have to imagine that while it's true that no one is immune to sin, attempting to live like Jesus sets us up pretty well for a good and fulfilling life.

My favorite television show is *The Bear*, not because I'm a Chicago Bears fan but because the main character profoundly resonates with me. Carmy was groomed for New York City restaurants, the next great chef with incredible staff, kitchens, cutlery, and the resources to get the best of the best foods for him to create with. Then his older brother died, so Carmy returned home to Chicago to take over his brother's Italian beef shop. It's filled with people who don't trust one another. They don't have the best of the best appliances or even sharp knives, and they are gravely understaffed.

But something happens in that kitchen that begins to transform him.

And that's what I'm discovering right now. I look back on the last 1,826 days and see a season of loss, the death of a dream in so many ways, the other shoe dropping after learning the truth of my father and past, and a man standing alone in the middle of the desert. That is part of the story, a valid part. A massive part. A part that has required care and tending and room for SPADURA and anger and more tears than I can count. It's not the whole story, though. Those five years of my life were also where I met myself in new ways. My faith changed and deepened. I became more of the husband and father I wanted to be and embraced a spiritual formation anchored in Jesus' life. I am not who I once was because grief changes us.

Do I regret running this race?

Never. I wouldn't change a thing.

When you look at your life, how would you answer that question? How do you feel as you reflect on the places where your grief has taken you and how it's changed you? The truth is, grief and difficulty aren't contained into five neat years.

Life is messy, always. Part of being alive means embracing the vulnerability and risk involved. There isn't a FastPass we can stamp to cut past the hard parts. The gold is found in what we uncover and discover during those painful experiences that make us who we are, show us what we want and don't want anymore, and invite us into a more authentic and courageous life.

The race you may find yourself in now might not resemble anything close to what you thought you were signing up for. In fact, you might be at a place in your life where you'd gladly accept a warm peanut butter sandwich from a stranger just to get some relief. I get it. But you're in it now, five miles down and eight more to go. I know you have what it takes to make it the rest of the way. I know there will be pain and ache waiting at the finish line, but there will also be recovery, care, and confidence in yourself that you can't begin to comprehend this side of the finish line.

Close your eyes and picture it: you, on the other side of your grief.

Strong. Healed. Brave.

Grateful. Confident. Unshakable.

Because Sunday is coming.

We run the race and become someone who embraces the possibility of hope.

First, we must *grieve*. Then we learn to *breathe* again. And from there, we can *receive* the new mercies God has for us.

Reflection Questions

1. What race are you running in your life right now?
2. When you picture yourself on the other side of your grief, what does it look like? How does it feel?
3. What is one new mercy you have received from God in this process? It can be as monumental or simple as you want, perhaps a moment in your GBR Journey when God met you and you knew you were not alone.

BENEDICTION

Growing up in Southern California, I learned how to surf at an early age. My friends and I would rush home after school and check the surf report, and if the waters weren't too choppy, we'd grab our boards and head toward the shore. Some days, the water would be so calm it would shimmer like glass reflecting the bright blue sky. Other days, the flags would be out, warning beachgoers to avoid the ocean, because riptides lurking under the surface made for exceptionally dangerous waters. But most days, the conditions were perfect: consistent sloping waves curling like clockwork, set after set, one on top of the other. It's not lost on me that waves are a preferred metaphor often connected to grief. Grief, like the ocean, is full of mystery and can be wild and dangerous as well as slow and calm. Water can wash us clean, nourish us, take us somewhere new, but it can also crush us, pulling us under with no hope of catching another breath.

So it is with grief.

As we've been on this GBR Journey together, there have been many moments of honest reflection, of asking the questions that lead to uncomfortable answers, of making room for sadness and anger and hope to take up their space within us. We've made decisions to let some things go, lightening our load, and we've also added some new practices to our packs. I imagine us now, coming to the end of the trail. Perhaps we're standing on the shoreline of our own stories, our own futures. I wonder what comes next for you. What happens when you step into the waters of hope that are lapping at your feet?

When I was in Portugal to hike the Camino, we spent one day at Nazaré Beach, a legendary spot known by surfers all over the world. These waves are literally killer and only the most professional and slightly insane surfers ever dare to ride them. I was so excited to see some incredible waves, but when we walked up to the cliff overlook, the waters were eerily calm. The sets were still. There was no drama. No thrill. Just quiet, pooling waters. I should have been disappointed, and in one way I was. But I was also really excited. Because I suddenly knew exactly why I'd come to the beach that day. I turned to my friend Tommy and asked him to baptize me. Was I already baptized? Yes. But it had been in the seventh grade and I'm pretty sure I wasn't able to grasp the full significance of what it represented for me at the time. Now, I was on the precipice of a new season for myself. I was stepping out of the 1,862 days my friend had referenced earlier in my journey. I was teetering between the first and second half of my life. I was coming out of a massive time of loss, and I was yearning to transition into a new season fresh with hope and something good. I didn't expect the moment I rose from the waters to change me. I knew there would be no dove, no fireworks moment, no thunderous clapping—but I also knew it would be a moment that would forever be significant to me. And it was.

And yet. Grief isn't something you just get through.

I was still in the midst of working out my grief, my anger, my confusion, my disillusionment. We humans tend to long for a Hollywood ending, something we can use to tie up our struggle with a bow, an explanation, something to make it all make sense. Those of us who have walked this journey, however, know better than that. We know firsthand that grief is less something we get through and more something we ride like those waves.

The Hebrew scriptures tell a fascinating story of Moses guiding a community of people who'd escaped a life of enslavement in Egypt through a desert on their way to freedom. At one point, he led them to the foot of Mount Sinai. Everything was covered in smoke; the Scriptures tell us this was because the Lord had descended as fire onto the mountaintop. Exodus 19:19 says that "Moses spoke and the voice of God answered him." There is a little footnote at the end of this verse in most Bibles that says, "or 'God answered him with thunder.'"

Some Jewish rabbis have a fascinating interpretation of this moment, suggesting that it wasn't the kind of thunder that accompanies a storm, all booms and lightning strikes.

No, they say this was more like a profound stirring from within, one that Moses would need to look inward to decipher. Essentially, he was going to have to translate the thunder. I have to say, there have definitely been times in my own GBR Journey when I've felt like God was asking me to learn a new language. There have for sure been moments when it felt like I was trying to translate the thunder of my loss and rage. Can you relate?

As we embrace our grief, as we learn to breathe again, and as we release control and learn to receive the gift of healing and hope, we slowly take the rumblings of our personal experiences and turn them into something beautiful. And in that, our grief is never wasted and our suffering is never for nothing. We are meaning-making a more beautiful interpretation for ourselves first, and then for every person on the planet who will someday experience grief, loss, and life doing what life often does.

One of my closest friends, Adam, recently said to me as he held these pages in his hands, "You don't journey *through* grief, you journey *with* grief."

That hits different when you've learned to grieve well. When you've chosen to honor what comes up when change shows up. When you walk those dusty desert grief trails breathing in and out. When you wait and wonder, feeling the SPADURA process under your skin. When you stop and rest, empty your pack, and remember to "travel lightly because you don't need as much as you think you do." When you realize that you are not standing still, being swallowed up by the enormity of your loss (although it can sometimes feel that way). No, you are transient, sometimes moving sideways and in circles, but always moving forward, closer to your hope and your peace.

My friend, thank you for coming with me. Thank you for letting me share and be honest, and messy, and sometimes a real bummer. Hopefully you felt safe and free and granted yourself permission to let your guard down, to settle in a little, to breathe deeply, to be honest with yourself. Hopefully, at some point you realized you are not alone, and while, yes, you are incredibly resilient for all that you've endured, you are also soft and brave and good. So very good. The loss we experience is a reflection of the love we've known, and the grief we express is merely a testament to the hope we have yet within us. May you trust the reality of Immanuel, that God is with you as you continue moving forward. May you trust yourself, the healing process as you embody the GBR Journey, and receive all the goodness that lies ahead for you.

Grace + Peace,
Steve Carter

ACKNOWLEDGMENTS

The last five years have been radically different than I ever anticipated, but God has surprised me with so much goodness along the journey. Incredible friends, mentors, communities, and partnerships have embodied the true meaning of integrity. In the legendary words of University of Michigan Football coach Bo Schembechler: "No man is more important than the team; no coach is more important than the team. The team, the team, the team!" And I am profoundly grateful for the team God has assembled to bring *Grieve, Breathe, Receive* into the world.

My home team:

Sarah, Emerson, and Mercy: I love you three more than anything! You are God's greatest gift to me, and these words would've never existed without your love and support.

The Bindery team:

Alexander Field: You're more than an agent; you have become a brother I deeply trust and respect. Thank you to the entire team at Bindery Agency for championing me and this book.

My W Publishing team:

Damon Reiss: Thank you for believing in the message of this book and reminding me to keep the faith and keep going.

Kyle Olund: Thanks for the many meals, conversations, and encouragement along the way—you are a gift, brother.

Rachel Buller: I am grateful for your steadfast diligence and brilliant editing skills—your commitment to your craft made this book better.

Lauren Ash and Elisabeth Hawkins: Thanks for all you did to help get the word out. So grateful for your care and creativity.

The Craft & Character podcast team:

Rob Toal and Todd Waterman: Thank you for believing in the redeeming value of a story like mine and for living with integrity in all you do.

Andrew Finch: Grateful for your Jedi wizardry in making the episodes get everywhere.

Toby Lyles: Where would I be without your genius-level production expertise?

Preaching Today: Thank you for the countless ways you've shown support along the way.

Food For the Hungry: I'm so honored to have been able to walk beside you on this journey; thanks for being along for the ride since day one.

Jordan Gustafson: I'll follow you anywhere. Thanks for being one of the good guys.

The Creative Design team:

Jeff Miller: The Faceout Studio squad is next level. Jeff, love what you did with this cover.

Jacob Titus and Kath Keur: Thank you to Bronson Strategy for the day in South Bend dreaming and the website you created around the heart of this book.

Forest City Church:

FCC staff, elders, and congregation: Thank you for welcoming me into your community and allowing me to join in what God is stirring in Elgin and Rockford, Illinois. It is an honor to serve God alongside each of you, and I genuinely believe the best is yet to come.

Mission Church, Faithbridge, and the Salvation Army:

Each of your congregations is so special to me, and I am humbled every time I get to be with you all.

To those who have walked with me in this desert season:

Journey Home: We need to run that Camino trip back. Something forever shifted within.

10ten project: Still can't get over all we experienced, shared, and the healing that happened.

Barbara: You are more than a therapist; you are a guide to freedom. I'll never forget that intensive.

Aaron Bartz: So many incredible adventures and conversations.

NOTES

INTRODUCTION
1. Dallas Willard, *The Spirit of the Disciplines: Understanding How God Changes Lives* (New York: HarperCollins, 1988).
2. September Vaudrey, *The Colors of Goodbye: A Memoir of Holding On, Letting Go, and Reclaiming Joy in the Wake of Loss* (Carol Stream, IL: Tyndale Momentum, 2016).

CHAPTER 1: 1,862 DAYS
1. Octavia E. Butler, *Parable of the Sower* (New York: Four Walls Eight Windows, 1993), 3.

CHAPTER 2: BORN IDENTITY
1. Manya Brachear Pashman and Jeff Coen, "After Years of Inquiries, Willow Creek Pastor Denies Misconduct Allegations," *Chicago Tribune*, March 23, 2018, https://www.chicagotribune.com/news/breaking/ct-met-willow-creek-pastor-20171220-story.html.
2. Speaker Christine Caine taught this concept when discussing a passage in Genesis 3 ("Who told you?").

CHAPTER 3: THE QUESTION
1. Laurie Goodstein, "He's a Superstar Pastor. She Worked for Him and Said He Groped Her Repeatedly," *New York Times*,

August 5, 2018, https://www.nytimes.com/2018/08/05/us
/bill-hybels-willow-creek-pat-baranowski.html.

2. "A Diverging Path," Steve Carter (blog post), August 5, 2018,
accessed September 11, 2023, https://stevecarter.org/a
-diverging-path/.

3. "Cadet's Prayer," *West Point Bugle Notes*, yearbook (West
Point, NY: Cadet Publications Program, US Military
Academy, 2021).

CHAPTER 4: SUBMARINE

1. Brené Brown, *Rising Strong: How the Ability to Reset
Transforms the Way We Live, Love, Parent, and Lead* (New
York: Random House, 2017), 4.

2. Joby Martin with Charles Martin, *If the Tomb Is Empty* (New
York: Faithwords/Hachette Book Group, 2022).

3. Andy Stanley, "Of First Importance," Sermons.love, June 12,
2023, https://sermons.love/andy-stanley/15187-andy-stanley
-of-first-importance.html.

4. Barbara Johnson, *Splashes of Joy in the Cesspools of Life*
(Nashville: Thomas Nelson, 1990), 193.

CHAPTER 5: SPADURA

1. Napoleon, who said, "The role of any leader is to define
reality and give hope."

2. Elisabeth Kübler-Ross, *On Death and Dying* (1964; reissue:
New York: Scribner, 2014).

3. "Natsar," Bible Hub entry, accessed September 12, 2023,
https://biblehub.com/hebrew/5341.htm.

CHAPTER 6: PUNCHING PILLOWS

1. For more information, visit https://www.10tenproject.com.

2. For more information, visit https://onsiteworkshops.com.

CHAPTER 7: STACKING STONES

1. Eugene H. Peterson, *Under the Unpredictable Plant: An Exploration in Vocational Holiness* (Grand Rapids: Eerdmans, 1992), 130.

CHAPTER 8: BET IT ALL

1. Anthony Cooley, "The Infamous Card Game: What Most Likely Happened," *White Mountain Independent*, December 28, 2016, https://www.wmicentral.com/news/local_news/the-infamous-card-game-what-most-likely-happened/article_312d5d04-c952–11e6-a487-d728797dcb10.html.
2. "What Did Jesus Do at Golgotha?" *Catholic World Today*, accessed September 13, 2023, https://saintleonards.org/theology/what-did-jesus-do-at-golgotha.html.

CHAPTER 9: SAVING FERRIS

1. For more information, see Bible Hub, "Barnes' Notes" for Luke 10:31, accessed September 13, 2023, https://biblehub.com/commentaries/barnes/luke/10.htm.
2. Roy B. Blizzard and David Bivin, "Study Shows Jesus as Rabbi," Bible Scholars, accessed January 5, 2024, https://www.biblescholars.org/2013/05/study-shows-jesus-as-rabbi.html.
3. "The Currency of Scarcity," March 18, 2020, on *The Home Team*, podcast, https://podcasters.spotify.com/pod/show/steve-carter2/episodes/The-Currency-of-Scarcity-eqtudi.
4. "Olympian Simone Biles Interviewed by Steve Carter at Willow Creek Community Church," video, February 13, 2018, https://stevecarter.org/video/olympian-simone-biles-interviewed-by-steve-carter-at-willow-creek-community-church/.

CHAPTER 10: CROSS + RELEASE

1. "Forgive/Forgiven–Aphiemi," Precept Austin (commentaries), updated March 6, 2023, https://www.preceptaustin.org /forgive-aphiemi-greek-word-study (accessed September 14, 2023).

2. Loren L. Toussaint, Grant S. Shields, and George M. Slavich, "Forgiveness, Stress, and Health: A 5-Week Dynamic Parallel Process Study," *Annals of Behavioral Medicine* (April 2016): 727–35, https://link.springer.com /article/10.1007/s12160–016–9796–6.

3. "Forgiveness: Your Health Depends on It," Johns Hopkins Medicine, https://www.hopkinsmedicine.org/health/wellness -and-prevention/forgiveness-your-health-depends-on-it #:~:text=%E2%80%9CThere%20is%20an%20enormous%20 physical,blood%20pressure%20and%20immune%20response.

4. "Forgive (Grant, Freely Give, Bestow) (5483) Charizomai," a text sermon on Greek word studies, Sermon Index.net, accessed September 14, 2023, https://www.sermonindex.net /modules/articles/index.php?view=article&aid=34100.

CHAPTER 11: FOUND AND LOST

1. *The Book of Mystical Chapters: Meditations on the Soul's Ascent from the Desert Fathers and Other Early Christian Contemplatives*, translated and introduced by John Anthony McGuckin (Boulder, CO: Shambhala Publications, 2002), 47.

2. "Headstone of Ruth Bell Graham . . . ," photographs in Carol M. Highsmith's America Project in the Carol M. Highsmith Archive, Library of Congress, Prints and Photographs Division, accessed September 15, 2023, https://www.loc.gov /item/2017880244.

3. "Hallelujah–Praise the Lord," Precept Austin (commentaries), November 7, 2022, https://www.preceptaustin.org/hallelujah -praise_the_lord.

CHAPTER 12: BREAKING BREAD

1. Dennis Green, postgame commentary, October 16, 2006, https://en.wikipedia.org/wiki/2006_Chicago_Bears–Arizona _Cardinals_game.
2. Jesuit priest once said, "We never take Eucharist; we only receive it. Taking is what the man and woman did in the garden. It's something many of us do in our everyday lives, we take and climb and strive to advance; but when it comes to Christ's bread, grace, and invitation, all we can ever do is simply receive and eat."

CHAPTER 14: YELLOW BUG

1. "Marrow Stem Cell Donor Matching Program Does Life-Saving Work," MLive, December 23, 2008, https://www .mlive.com/living/grand-rapids/2008/12/marrowstem_cell _donor_matching.html.

CHAPTER 15: HOMECOMING

1. Alice Miller, *The Drama of the Gifted Child: The Search for the True Self* (1979; repr., New York: Basic Books, 2008).
2. Daniel Grothe, *The Power of Place: Choosing Stability in a Rootless Age* (Nashville: Thomas Nelson, 2021).

ABOUT THE AUTHOR

Steve Carter is the bestselling author of *The Thing Beneath the Thing*, host of the *Craft & Character* podcast, and a personal coach to communicators discovering their unique voice and taking their skills to the next level. He currently serves as a teaching pastor at Forest City Church and teaches regularly at churches, conferences, and various businesses worldwide. Steve currently lives outside Chicago, Illinois, with his wife and two kids. When he's not hanging with his family and friends or working, you will probably find him cheering on his favorite team, the University of Michigan.

Steve Carter creates inspiring content to help people
discover what grace + peace is all about. Check out
SteveCarter.org to learn more about his books,
small group resources for *Grieve, Breathe, Receive*,
the *Craft & Character* podcast, speaking events,
and executive coaching.